Praise for *Tear Down This Wall*

"Fast-moving and splendidly written. . . . Mr. Ratnesar's book, based on interviews with former Reagan administration officials, American and German eyewitnesses who were present at the event, State Department documents and East German records, gives us both an accurate and detailed picture of our cumbersome governmental policymaking process and a remarkable re-creation of the last days of the Soviet empire, with East Germany as the culmination of the Marxist dialectic, and the wall the perfect symbol for that strange alternate universe."

—John R. Coyne, Jr., *Washington Times*

"I hated to see it end. . . . It isn't just the story of a speech, but a lesson in communicating from the man known as the Great Communicator."

—Dale Dauten, *Arizona Daily Star*

"Capture[s] the essence of those heady days leading up to a new world order."

—*Newark Morning Ledger*

"A lively, impressively detailed history of the iconic speech . . . readers should enjoy this slim, lucid account of a time when events turned out brilliantly."

—*Publishers Weekly*

"[Ratnesar] captures the full historical context and bricks-and-mortar development of Ronald Reagan's memorable yet controversial 1987 speech at the Berlin Wall. His presentation of the recollections of residents of East and West Berlin at the time vividly shows how controlling the East German Communist government and its secret police were in monitoring East Germans and trying (yet often failing) to shield them from Western political and cultural influence . . . Ratnesar's portrayal of Gorbachev is also first rate. . . . This book may be read with pleasure by many, from trained historians to curious general readers."

—*Library Journal*

"Capably portrays the nuts-and-bolts process of crafting a presidential speech. . . . Ratnesar widens his scope, effectively placing the speech in the context of the Cold War. . . . A well balanced look at a key moment in Reagan's presidency."

—*Kirkus Reviews*

"Provides useful insights into the evolving personal relationships between Reagan and Gorbachev . . . offers a valuable interpretation of the political and diplomatic maneuvers on both sides."

—*Booklist*

"Romesh Ratnesar has written a smart and deeply illuminating history of Ronald Reagan at the zenith of the Cold War. *Tear Down This Wall* helps clarify a lot of misnomers about Reagan's most enduring speech. This is a fine, important, and admirable study. Highly recommended!"

—Douglas Brinkley, author of *Wilderness Warrior*

"Among the fascinating challenges facing historians are figuring out how Ronald Reagan's mind worked and assessing the factors that led to the end of the Cold War. Romesh Ratnesar weaves these together brilliantly. This is an exciting narrative that explains a critical moment in history and brings to life the amazing players in a great drama."

—Walter Isaacson, author of *Einstein*

"The four words that Ronald Reagan hurled at Mikhail Gorbachev were an exhortation, even a demand, but they were also part of a dialogue, a partnership, and a friendship that changed the world. It is high time for a focused study of how that speech came to be written and why it was so consequential. Romesh Ratnesar has told the story with narrative verve, brilliant political and personal insight, and a combination of concision and pithiness worthy of the Great Communicator himself."

—Strobe Talbott, author of *The Great Experiment*

"More than most presidents, Ronald Reagan governed through his speeches—never to greater effect than in his 1987 Berlin summons to 'Tear down this wall.' With the perspective of time, access to newly available papers, and a Reaganesque flair for storytelling with a point, Romesh Ratnesar gives us the ultimate insider's account of the history that unfolded when those around him, sometimes reluctantly, let Reagan be Reagan. No future discussion of the Cold War and how it ended will be complete without reference to this riveting book."

—Richard Norton Smith, author of *The Colonel*

TEAR
DOWN
THIS
WALL

Simon & Schuster Paperbacks

A City,
a President,
and the Speech
That Ended the
Cold War

ROMESH
RATNESAR

NEW YORK LONDON TORONTO SYDNEY

PHOTO CREDITS

Photo by Yevgeny Khaldei: 1
U.S. Army Signal Corps, courtesy of Harry S. Truman Library: 2
U.S. Air Force: 3
Photo by Peter Leibing: 4
Associated Press: 5
Courtesy of Ronald Reagan Library: 6, 7, 8, 9, 10, 11, 12, 13, 14
ALIMDI.NET / N. Michalke: 15

Simon & Schuster Paperbacks
A Division of Simon & Schuster, Inc.
1230 Avenue of the Americas
New York, NY 10020

First Simon & Schuster trade paperback edition November 2010

SIMON & SCHUSTER PAPERBACKS and colophon are registered
trademarks of Simon & Schuster, Inc.

For information about special discounts for bulk purchases,
please contact Simon & Schuster Special Sales at
1-866-506-1949 or business@simonandschuster.com.

The Simon & Schuster Speakers Bureau can bring authors
to your live event. For more information or to book an event
contact the Simon & Schuster Speakers Bureau at
1-866-248-3049 or visit our website at www.simonspeakers.com.

Text designed by Paul Dippolito

Manufactured in the United States of America

1   3   5   7   9   10   8   6   4   2

The Library of Congress has cataloged the hardcover edition as follows:
Ratnesar, Romesh
Tear down this wall : a city, a president, and the speech that ended
the Cold War / Romesh Ratnesar.
p. cm.
1. Reagan, Ronald—Oratory.   2. Reagan, Ronald—Political and social views.
3. Speeches, addresses, etc., American—Germany—Berlin.
4. Berlin Wall, Berlin, Germany, 1961–1989.   5. Gorbachev,
Mikhail Sergeevich, 1931–   6. United States—Foreign relations—
Soviet Union.   7. Soviet Union—Foreign relations—United States.
8. Cold War   I. Title.
E877.2.R38 2009
973.927092—dc22   2009024213

ISBN 978-1-4165-5690-9
ISBN 978-1-4165-5691-6 (pbk)
ISBN 978-1-4391-7005-2 (e-book)

To my parents

CONTENTS

INTRODUCTION

The morning of May 15, 1987, was a busy one for Ronald Reagan. "Quite an agenda," he recorded in the diary he updated every day of his presidency. He reviewed names of possible appointees to a commission on AIDS—the disease that was claiming tens of thousands of lives but which Reagan had only recently acknowledged. At a meeting of the National Security Council, Reagan found his disputatious secretaries of state and defense, George Shultz and Caspar Weinberger, feuding over whether the United States should agree to a major arms cut proposal made by the Soviet Union's leader, Mikhail Gorbachev. Reagan was also informed that a U.S. Army nurse had been kidnapped in Mozambique. "I want her rescued if we have to blow up the whole d——m country," he wrote later. After lunch and a meeting with regional newspaper journalists, the seventy-six-year-old president retired "upstairs for the afternoon and evening," with a stack of material to read over the weekend. Among his papers were drafts of the speeches he was to deliver on an upcoming trip to Europe—including one he would be giving on June 12 in West Germany, in the shadow of the Berlin Wall.

Even to some who knew him well, Reagan was a remote figure. His basic kindness and decency were obvious to all he encountered, but so were his emotional reserve and imperviousness to events that might disrupt his simple, sunny worldview. During his time in the White House, he rarely budged from a daily routine that included a lunch of soup and crackers, a light workout, and eight hours of sleep. On the morning of Reagan's first inauguration, the man he had defeated, Jimmy Carter, received word that fifty-two American hostages, held in Tehran for 444 days, were to be released. When Carter phoned to give Reagan the news, an aide to Reagan, Michael Deaver, told the outgoing president that Reagan was sleeping and couldn't be roused. "You're kidding," Carter said. "No, I'm not," Deaver replied. By the final years of his second term, Reagan was often disengaged from the daily business of the presidency. His official biographer observed at the time that Reagan was "showing signs of depression, failing to read even summaries of important work papers, constantly watching TV and the movies." Reagan's celebrated speechwriter, Peggy Noonan, told an interviewer that when she met with Reagan before she left the White House in 1986, she had been struck most by his "frailty." "He nods and encourages you," she said, "but you're never quite sure he hears every word."

But Reagan could still rise to the occasion. "He believed that giving speeches was one of the president's most important duties," says James Baker, who served under Reagan as chief of staff and later as treasury secretary. "I've never known a president who was better at utilizing the bully pulpit, which is the most important thing that a president has." Reagan's gift for public speaking had been evident as far back as his days at Eureka College, when his peers tapped him as their spokesman during a student strike against the school president. That talent was honed by thousands of commentaries, radio broadcasts, town hall meetings, and fund-raising speeches Reagan gave before he even mounted his first campaign for office in 1966. His detractors confused Reagan's eloquence with glibness, dismissing his ability to connect with audiences as an old actor's trick. But those judgments now seem hollow; heard today, Reagan's best speeches—"Evil Empire," the elegy for the crew of the space shuttle Challenger, "The Boys of Pointe du Hoc"—retain much of their rhetorical power. Reagan approached speeches not merely as public performances but as opportunities to present his views in clear and unmistakable terms. Even his closest aides said they often learned about Reagan's position on a given issue only after he mentioned it in a speech. Former President Gerald Ford once remarked in wonder that Reagan "was one of the few political leaders I have met whose public speeches revealed more than his private conversations."

The address delivered by Reagan in West Berlin on June 12, 1987, was the 1,279th of his presidency. He was entering the twilight of his tenure. His long love affair with the American people had soured over the Iran-contra scandal. His approval rating had fallen twenty points in six months. On the world stage too, Reagan appeared a diminished figure, overshadowed by the dynamic Soviet leader, Gorbachev, whose push to reform the communist system seemed to be driving the course of history. In two dramatic summits to that point, Reagan and Gorbachev had established a promising personal connection, but their discussions had failed to yield tangible progress toward ending their nations' rivalry. At their summit in Reykjavik, Iceland, in October 1986, the two leaders had come tantalizingly close to reaching an agreement to eliminate nuclear weapons, before the deal fell apart over Reagan's refusal to abandon his plan to build a space-based defense against nuclear missiles. Few experts in either country believed the Cold War was about to end.

But the world was changing. In Eastern Europe, small-scale rebellions against communist rule had begun to stir. On the eve of Reagan's visit, hundreds of East German youths revolted near the Berlin Wall when police tried to prevent them from listening to a rock concert in West Berlin. Whether the American president sensed the ground moving, or merely allowed himself to imagine it, is difficult to know. As Reagan climbed the dais in front of Berlin's

Brandenburg Gate just after 2 P.M. on June 12, 1987, it is unlikely
that he anticipated that by the end of the year he and Gorbachev
would sign the first U.S-Soviet treaty to reduce nuclear weapons;
that he would leave office in January 1989 declaring that "the Cold
War is over"; and that just nine months would pass after that before
the fall of the Berlin Wall.

And even the man known as the Great Communicator might
not have believed, on that gray Berlin afternoon, that his words
would become the most memorable delivered by any American
president in the last quarter-century. Along with the assassination
attempt against him in 1981, Reagan's appearance at the Brandenburg Gate remains the iconic image of his presidency. During the
2008 presidential campaign, *Time* named "Remarks on East-West
Relations at the Brandenburg Gate" one of the ten best political
speeches in history. *USA Today* rated "Tear down this Wall" the second most memorable quote of the last twenty-five years.* "You look
for one line you remember a president by," says Ken Duberstein,
a former White House chief of staff who accompanied Reagan on
that day in Berlin. "FDR is easy. Bill Clinton is easy: 'I did not have
sex with that woman.' What is Ronald Reagan going to be remembered by? One line: Tear down this Wall."

Twenty years since the fall of the Berlin Wall, it is sometimes
difficult for Americans to recall the antagonism, bitterness, and
depredation that characterized the Cold War. For more than four
decades, the United States and Soviet Union remained locked in a
struggle, in President George H. W. Bush's words, "for the soul of
mankind." It was a conflict that distorted national priorities and led
both countries into disastrous misadventures; hundreds of thousands died in the proxy conflicts waged by the superpowers around

---

* "Let's Roll," the phrase immortalized by Todd Beamer, a passenger on United
Flight 93—which was hijacked on September 11, 2001, and crashed in Shanksville,
Pennsylvania—came in first.

the globe. Wars against communist foes in Korea and Vietnam claimed the lives of more than 100,000 American troops. For millions living under communism in Eastern Europe and the Soviet Union, the price of the Cold War was paid in the form of dismal health standards, diminished life expectancy, an absence of political freedom, and the crushing of individual will. And due to the U.S.-Soviet arms race, for half a century the world lived with the specter of nuclear war, a hair's-trigger away from Armageddon.

In this contest of wills, Berlin was the most visible staging ground. Divided into four sectors by the conquering Allies after World War II, the city came to embody the contrast between two competing ideologies: the vibrant, market-oriented democracy of the West versus the gray, statist socialism of the East. The Berlin Wall, built by the communists in 1961, was the Cold War's defining symbol. Stretching over 100 miles, reinforced with concrete, barbed wire, and dog runs, the Wall literally separated brother from brother, neighbor from neighbor, and block from block. During the twenty-eight-year existence of the Berlin Wall, at least two hundred East Germans were killed and another five thousand captured while trying to cross it. Symbolically, the Wall stood for the mistrust that plagued East-West relations during the postwar period.

Reagan loathed the Wall. On a trip to West Berlin in 1978, he was taken to an eighth-floor office overlooking it and told the story of Peter Fechter, the youth who had been gunned down by East German police in 1962 as he tried to crawl over. The authorities left Fechter unattended for nearly an hour, while he bled to death. "Reagan just gritted his teeth when he heard all of this," says Peter Hannaford, a longtime aide who was with Reagan that day. "You could tell from the set of his jaw and his look and some of the things he said that . . . he was very, very determined that this was something that had to go."

Reagan's speechwriters knew this. From the start of the administration, they viewed themselves as the keepers of the flame of the

Reagan revolution. The presidential trip to West Berlin in June 1987, which came on the occasion of the city's 750th birthday, presented an opportunity to create one last signature moment for the aging president. "We understood that this was what we had all been working for. It was going to be *the* speech of the Cold War," says Dana Rohrabacher, a veteran Reagan speechwriter who would later become an eleven-term congressman. The writer assigned to the speech, Peter Robinson, had begun drafting it in April, after a scouting trip to Berlin. His early drafts included the line "Herr Gorbachev, bring down this wall." Though the syntax was clumsy, the message grabbed Reagan. "That wall has to come down," he told the speechwriters in a twenty-one-minute meeting in the Oval Office. Over the next three weeks, the speech—and specifically, the direct challenge to Gorbachev to tear down the Wall—became the subject of intense debate among Reagan's national security team. Secretary of State George Shultz, chief of staff Howard Baker, and General Colin Powell, then the deputy national security adviser, all lobbied for the draft to be scrapped, arguing that it would embarrass Gorbachev and play into the hands of Kremlin hard-liners. Years later, Robinson wrote that "What State and NSC were saying, in effect, was that the President could go ahead and issue a call for the destruction of the Wall—but only if he employed language so vague and euphemistic that everybody could see right away he didn't mean it."

The truth is more complicated. This book is devoted to reconstructing Reagan's "Tear Down This Wall" address, the context in which it was given and its ultimate place in history. It is based on interviews with former Reagan administration officials as well as journalists, historians, and numerous eyewitnesses to the speech in the United States and Germany. It also draws on primary source material rarely examined before, including declassified State Department documents and East German records of the president's trip, now kept in the archives of the former East Germany in Berlin. A close examination of the history of the speech reveals texture and shadings often missing from previous accounts, including those of the main participants. And it clears up misconceptions—among them the claim, promoted by some of Reagan's admirers, that by calling for the Berlin Wall to be removed, the president was defying the prevailing wisdom inside his own administration. In fact, Reagan's call reflected a growing view among U.S. policymakers that the time had come to pressure the Soviets to liberate Berlin.

The portrait of Reagan that emerges is more complex too. To both his critics and champions, Reagan's address reflected the qualities that defined him in the public imagination—idealism touched with naïveté, rhetorical toughness verging on cowboy posturing. With the benefit of two decades of reflection, it is possible to read the speech in a different way: as an open gesture to Gorbachev, an attempt to move beyond the enmities of the past by pointing him to a different future. Listen closely to a recording of it: the speech is as much an invitation as it is a challenge. "There is one sign the Soviets can make that would be unmistakable, that would advance dramatically the cause of freedom and peace," Reagan says. As he goes on, you hear scattered claps and hollers. "General Secretary Gorbachev, if you seek peace, if you seek prosperity for the Soviet Union and Eastern Europe, if you seek liberalization: Come here to this gate!" Reagan entreats. The cheers grow. "Mr. Gorbachev, open this gate!" Reagan would later say that as he gave the speech, he felt anger at the East German authorities for preventing people in East Berlin from hearing it.* Though the Soviets dismissed the speech as "openly provocative, war-mongering," history has proven

---

* Reagan claimed in an interview in 1989 that he had watched police push crowds in East Berlin back from the Wall shortly before his speech. In fact, the authorities had blockaded the perimeter near the Brandenburg Gate the night before. While about two hundred East Germans headed to the Unter den Linden for the Reagan speech, they could get no closer than a half-mile from the Brandenburg Gate. It is highly unlikely Reagan actually saw them.

Reagan farsighted. "In this age of redoubled economic growth, of information and innovation, the Soviet Union faces a choice," he said later in the speech. "It must make fundamental changes, or it will become obsolete."

That remark echoed Reagan's prediction, made in a 1982 address to the British Parliament, that the West would leave the communist system "on the ash heap of history." But the Reagan who arrived in Berlin in the summer of 1987 was a different president. The historian Sean Wilentz observed that "[Reagan's] dare to Gorbachev, by even mentioning peace and liberalization, showed how much his rhetoric had changed since his denunciation of the Soviet Union four years earlier as 'the focus of evil in the modern world.'"

What did Reagan hope to achieve in Berlin? How did those who heard the speech react to it? How much did the speech contribute to the toppling of the Wall and the ultimate collapse of communism? In his diary Reagan wrote that he "addressed tens & tens of thousands of people—stretching as far as the eye could see. I got a tremendous reception—interrupted 28 times by cheers." Coverage of the speech led the three network-news broadcasts that night, but did not make the front page of the *New York Times*. *Time* called it a "strong performance" but "not quite enough to erase the impression that Reagan is losing the initiative to his Soviet rival." The speech failed to generate much excitement among Reagan aides like National Security Adviser Frank Carlucci, who saw it firsthand. "I remember thinking to myself, 'It's a great speech line. But it'll never happen.'"

Just two years later, it did. But how? Though largely overlooked at the time of the speech, it was the relationship that Reagan was forging with Gorbachev that ultimately defused the Cold War. If some of Reagan's advisers fretted that personally calling on Gorbachev to tear down the Wall might offend the Soviet leader, Reagan was convinced it might actually inspire him. "If he took down that Wall, he'd win the Nobel Prize," Reagan told an aide after returning home from Berlin. The confidence Reagan and Gorbachev had in each other allowed them finally to overcome the suspicions that stymied their predecessors. In that respect, the "Tear Down This Wall" speech marked, if not the end of the Cold War, then the beginning of the end.

For a politician, Reagan could be remarkably guileless. He actually believed what he said. And far more than those around him, Reagan recognized the power of words. That is a quality he shared with the two other great presidential orators of the last century: Franklin D. Roosevelt and John F. Kennedy. The journalist James Fallows writes that Roosevelt, Kennedy, and Reagan "all magnified their power . . . through their ability to explain what they were trying to do. 'The only thing we have to fear . . . ,' 'Ask not . . . ,' 'Tear down this Wall'—such phrases changed people's minds and shaped events." Rare is the speech that alters history on its own. But the ones we remember manage, if only through a single phrase, to capture the characters and principles of the presidents who deliver them. They are windows into their minds.

In his book on Kennedy's first inaugural address, *Ask Not*, Thurston Clarke wrote that "Every great speech is supposed to express a great idea." The ideas running through Reagan's speech in Berlin remained remarkably consistent throughout his public life: Change is possible. The human spirit is indomitable. Freedom triumphs. Reagan was also building on a broad foundation laid down over the course of four decades. The American commitment to a free Berlin—and beyond it, a free and undivided Europe—stretched back to the earliest, treacherous days of the postwar period, when during the Berlin Airlift, Harry Truman resolved not to allow the city to fall into Soviet hands. If that commitment wavered on occasion over the years, it never broke. It is not an exaggeration to say that the support of generations of Americans helped enable the people of Berlin to take back their city, tear down the Wall and deal the decisive blow to communist rule in Europe.

On November 10, 1989, the day after the Wall came down, West German chancellor Helmut Kohl spoke by phone to Reagan's successor, George H. W. Bush. "Without the U.S. this day would not have been possible," Kohl said, telling Bush that Germans gathered at the Brandenburg Gate had roared in appreciation when Kohl thanked America. The peaceful end of the Cold War and the unification of Europe stand as the high-water mark of U.S. foreign policy in the second half of the twentieth century. Ronald Reagan's speech at the Brandenburg Gate was indispensable to that achievement. But it is only part of the story.

1. BETTER THAN A WAR

H arry S. Truman gazed out at the open waters of the
Atlantic Ocean from his cabin aboard the USS *Augusta*
on July 7, 1945. "How I hate this trip!" he wrote in his
diary. Eight days later the president arrived in Potsdam, Germany,
fifteen miles outside Berlin, to meet Winston Churchill and Josef
Stalin to discuss the shape of the postwar world. On the three-and-
a-half-hour flight from Brussels to Berlin, Truman viewed an apoc-
alyptic landscape of wrecked roads and bridges, burning debris and
corpses strewn across the German countryside. "You who have not
seen it do not know what hell looks like from the top," George
Patton later said. In Potsdam, Truman stayed at 2 Kaiserstrasse, a
three-story villa that had belonged to the head of the Nazi movie
industry. Churchill and Truman met privately at 11 A.M. on the
morning of July 15, but Stalin was delayed and the opening of the
conference was postponed. And so on the afternoon of the 16th
Truman decided to tour Berlin.

Death hung over the city. Truman, riding in an open-top Lincoln, found the stench of rotting corpses nearly overwhelming. At
least fifty thousand people had been killed by the Allied bombing campaign that finally crushed the Third Reich. Some 35,000
children were left orphaned. On the roads into the city Truman's
motorcade passed lines of homeless, hungry Germans, who barely

acknowledged the conquering president, if they recognized him at all. The main avenues of the German capital, which had been the seat of Nazi power, were unrecognizable. Truman passed the Tiergarten, the city's central park, then traveled along the Unter den Linden, Berlin's once graceful boulevard, toward the Brandenburg Gate. The Red Army had bulldozed the lime trees along the Unter den Linden and hung the hammer-and-sickle from the ruins of the Reichstag. Rubble was everywhere. "I have never seen such destruction," Truman wrote that evening in his diary.

The shaken president had been on the job for less than three months. "I thought of Carthage, Baalbek, Jerusalem, Rome, Atlantis, Peking," Truman wrote that night. "But I fear that machines are ahead of morals by some centuries and when morals catch up there'll be no reason for any of it." Truman never doubted the rightness of the war against Hitler—"They brought it on themselves," he said when his car had pulled up to the bomb-blasted Chancellery, where Hitler killed himself—but his mind was filled with excitement and apprehension. He knew that the U.S.'s secret project to build an atomic bomb was nearing its completion. Earlier that day, at an air base in Alamogordo, New Mexico, the United States had conducted the first successful test of the bomb. For all three leaders at Potsdam, the new weapon would profoundly affect their considerations over the future of Europe—and the ruined city that lay at its heart, Berlin.

A fishing town built on soil irrigated by the waters of the Spree River, Berlin (the names comes from the Slavic term for "marsh") became a home to German monarchs in the fifteenth century. The first three hundred years of the city's history were marked by bursts of rebellion, war, disease, and plunder. In 1806, Napoleon entered Berlin with 25,000 French troops, parading through the recently constructed Brandenburg Gate, a neoclassical structure topped with a stone sculpture of a four-horse chariot, which Napoleon's men promptly packed off to Paris. After the unification of Germany in 1870, Berlin flourished into a modern metropolis, under the hand of the country's founding father, Otto von Bismarck. By 1900, the city's population was two million, the fourth largest in Europe. The city's rapid development and embrace of modern engineering—as early as 1870, Berlin had a steam railway, and by 1902 all of its trolley lines had gone electric—led Mark Twain to call it "the German Chicago." Lenin said, "He who controls Berlin controls Germany. And he who controls Germany controls Europe."

Germany's defeat in World War I stunted Berlin's development. As the historian David Clay Large wrote, Berliners during the war subsisted on ersatz foods—ash disguised as pepper, a butter consisting of a mix of soda and starch—as well as rats, cats, and dead horses. At the same time, "the city's cultural industry profited from people's need for distraction." Intellectuals and artists like Franz Kafka, Bertolt Brecht, and Vladimir Nabokov settled in Berlin during the interwar years. Even Albert Einstein, who had risen to international prominence for his general theory of relativity, vowed "not to turn my back on Berlin."

To many, postwar Berlin was a hothouse of cultural ferment and social freedom; to others, like the Nazi leader Adolf Hitler, the city reeked of corruption and decay. "A sink hole of iniquity," Joseph Goebbels wrote after spending a night in Berlin. In a weekly column published in the Nazi Party's newspaper, Goebbels laid blame for the city's "repulsive pseudoculture" on its Jewish residents. Playing on anti-Jewish bigotry and public discontent with high unemployment, the Nazis built their strength in Berlin. When Adolf Hitler assumed the chancellorship on January 30, 1933, Nazi Party members celebrated their victory with a torchlight procession through the Brandenburg Gate. The Nazis launched a campaign to harass, demonize, and expel Jews, who in 1933 made up nearly 4 percent of Berlin's population. By 1940, only seventy thousand Jews still lived in Berlin. On October 14, 1941, on the order of Goebbels, the deportation of all remaining Jews from the city began. More than fifty thousand Jews were forcibly deported over the next four years. At least 35,000 ended up in Auschwitz.

Lulled into a false security after Germany annexed Czechoslovakia, invaded Poland, and blitzed London, Berliners began to feel the brunt of war in the summer of 1943, as the Allies pounded the city with explosive and incendiary bombs. By 1944 nearly a quarter of the city's population was homeless. Tens of thousands of Berliners were killed. Led by General Dwight D. Eisenhower, Allied ground forces crossed the Rhine and advanced across the center and south of Germany, while the Soviet army blasted their way toward Berlin from the east, reaching the outskirts of the capital on April 19, 1945. On April 30, with Soviet tanks leveling the city center, Hitler committed suicide with his wife, Eva Braun. Nazi officers doused the bodies with gasoline and set them on fire, then buried them under a thin layer of dirt. On May 2, Red Army troops entered Berlin and raised the Soviet flag over the Reichstag. The war was over.

Berlin's ordeal was not. It took another two months for U.S. and British troops to arrive in the capital; in the meantime, Red Army soldiers engaged in rape and plunder. All of Berlin's major cultural treasures were stripped and sent to museums in the Soviet Union. The worst suffering was visited on German women. In their zone of occupation the Russians raped women as young as ten and as old as seventy, some as many as sixty times. U.S. and British troops entering that July found survivors as thoroughly traumatized as they were desperate. "Anything human in these indescribable ruins must exist in an unknown form," wrote a U.S. political officer named Hans Speier. "Seeing the survivors you almost hope they are not human."

This was the city that awaited Truman at the start of the Potsdam Conference. Germany dominated the early plenary discussions among Truman, Stalin, and Churchill and their aides, held around a circular conference table covered in burgundy cloth.

A few points were established: Germany would be demilitarized and broken into four occupied zones; war criminals would be punished; and the occupying powers would regulate Germany's industrial output. Berlin was divided into four pie-shaped sectors, each controlled by one of the conquering Allies—United States, Britain, France, and the Soviet Union. Stalin told Truman at the beginning of the conference that while he wanted to cooperate with the U.S. in war and in peace, the latter would be more difficult. Truman was "more sure of himself, more assertive," in the historian David McCullough's words, with the knowledge of the successful atomic test. On July 24, Truman and Churchill agreed that the bomb would be used against Japan. That afternoon Truman informed Stalin that the United States had "a new weapon of unusual destructive force." Stalin shrugged. Since 1943, the German-born physicist Klaus Fuchs had been passing information about the Manhattan Project to the Soviets. Stalin had known about the bomb for years.

However emboldened he may have felt, Truman secured few major concessions at Potsdam. The Allies agreed on the ambiguous goals of "democratization, denazification, and decartelization" of German society. But key issues pertaining to the future of Germany—such as Western access to Berlin, which lay in the Soviet zone of occupation, and what reparations the powers could extract from their respective zones—were kicked down the road. The failure to resolve those issues would result in Germany's division. But Truman had other things on his mind. He still needed Stalin's help to finish the war against Japan—at the time, Truman believed that a land invasion would still be necessary to compel Japan's surrender. The world was tired of war, the president told his wife. Truman wanted peace. He was willing to work with Stalin, despite the Soviet leader's monstrous rule. Stalin's shrewd intelligence impressed Truman. "I liked the little son-of-a-bitch," he said.

Truman made only one speech in Berlin. On July 20, he spoke

at the raising of the flag over the new headquarters of the U.S. military command. The flag had flown over the U.S. Capitol on the day the U.S. declared war on Germany. Shortly before 4 P.M. he spoke in the courtyard of the headquarters building. At his side were General George Patton, commander of the U.S. Third Army, General Lucius Clay, Eisenhower's deputy, and Secretary of War Henry Stimson. Clay wrote that "I have never forgotten that short ceremony as our flag rose to the staff." The president's voice filled with emotion as he delivered his short remarks, without notes. "We want peace and prosperity for the world as a whole," he said. "We want to see the time come when we can do things in peace that we have been able to do in war." If the might that had defeated Hitler's Germany could be harnessed to work for peace, then "we can look forward to the greatest age in the history of mankind."

Despite the soaring vision of Truman's words, millions across Europe remained on the edge of survival. The average German adult at the start of the war consumed 2,445 calories per day. In 1945–1946 he consumed 1,412; in the American zone of occupied Berlin the average ration was less than nine hundred calories. U.S. and British authorities feared that such privation might make ordinary Germans more receptive to communism, or even a revived Nazism. But the destruction of German industry, and the continued extraction of reparations (the lion's share by the Soviets, who also claimed the right to 10 percent of reparations from the Western zones) meant the country was unable to stand on its own.

Truman, his secretary of state, George Marshall, and British foreign minister Ernest Bevin believed that Europe's recovery was impossible without the rehabilitation of Germany. In 1947, the United States and Britain fused the economies of their zones. At a meeting of foreign ministers in Moscow the following year, the Western allies rebuffed the Soviets' demand to establish a single German administration and economy, which they saw as an attempt to pull Germany into the Soviet orbit. A directive by the U.S. Joint Chiefs formally laid out the new aims of unifying the Western zones of Germany and promoting self-government there.

On June 1, 1948, the Western allies announced their plans to create a separate West German state. Three weeks later, they introduced a new currency in their zones, the deutschmark. In turn the Soviets introduced their own mark in eastern Germany, including Berlin. When Western military officials voided that move and issued the western deutschmark in their sectors of the city, the Soviets responded by closing the road and rail route linking West Berlin to the rest of the country.

The blockade left 2.5 million people in the Allied sectors of Berlin without access to water, food, or fuel supplies. U.S. and British forces could bring in reinforcements only by air. Stalin wanted to force the Allies either to withdraw from Berlin or abandon their plans for a separate state. "We stay in Berlin, period," Truman told his aides on June 24. On June 29 he ordered that supplies be airlifted into West Berlin. Flying into and out of Tempelhof Airport, U.S. and British planes delivered 2.3 million tons of food to the besieged city over the next eleven months. At the peak of the airlift, a plane landed every ninety seconds in West Berlin. Seventy-three Allied airmen died conducting the airlift, which ended when Stalin lifted the blockade in May 1949. The airlift made the U.S. pilots heroes and turned West German opinion solidly against Stalin and toward the United States. "The Russians no longer scoff at the airlift," a reporter traveling aboard one of the relief planes wrote at the time. "As for the Germans they see democracy in action in the air; and they like what they see."

Stalin's bid to prevent the establishment of a separate West German government failed. In April 1949, France joined the Anglo-American zone, increasing the population of West Germany to 49 million, compared to 17 million in the east. The next month, the Federal Republic of Germany came into being. Four months later the communists established the German Democratic Republic in the east. Berlin's political and legal status was ambiguous. Residents of West Berlin became citizens of the Federal Republic, and East Berliners were absorbed into the GDR. But the city remained under the authority of the Four Powers for the next half century.

With the country formally divided, the Allies focused on rebuilding the West German economy. From 1949 to 1954, West Germany received $29 per capita in aid money from the Marshall Plan. By the early 1950s, with the West German economy thriving, Washington no longer viewed the unification of Germany as urgent. Stalin proposed a treaty that would establish a single German state, with a democratically elected central government and all occupying forces withdrawn. The Allies rejected the idea, still wary that the Soviet military's conventional superiority would allow it to dominate a demilitarized Germany. A month after Stalin's death in March 1953, President Eisenhower expressed support for the idea of German unification, provided Moscow made concessions on other issues. But with the Kremlin in the midst of a leadership struggle, Eisenhower's proposal went nowhere. It would take decades before unification became a viable prospect again.

The communist-run state in East Germany lacked popular support. From 1947 to 1952, the standard of living of ordinary East Germans declined. Hundreds of thousands crossed the "border" into the West. In June 1953, Walter Ulbricht, the first secretary of the ruling Socialist Unity Party, provoked riots when he declared that all workers would be required to do 10 percent more work. More than 100,000 people from all over East Germany converged on Potsdamer Platz in Berlin, destroying state-owned shops, burning government offices, and demanding elections. When the protesters tried to clamber onto one of the Soviet T-34 tanks that had been deployed to the city center, the Russians opened fire. In all,

East German police and soldiers killed 267 of their own people and seriously injured 1,067.

The uprising raised alarms in Moscow. In the absence of economic improvement, maintaining internal security and stamping out dissent became essential to the survival of the GDR. Millions of East Germans still fled to the West; in its first twelve years of existence, East Germany lost nearly 20 percent of its population. Hoping to reverse the tide, Soviet premier Nikita Khrushchev held a news conference in Moscow on November 27, 1958, Thanksgiving Day in the U.S. He demanded that Berlin become a "free city," that Allied forces withdraw from it and sign a German peace treaty within six months. Khrushchev wanted to use Berlin as a bargaining chip to force the Western powers to recognize the division of Germany. By doing so, Khrushchev could proclaim the legitimacy of his East German client, stabilize Eastern Europe, and forestall the military buildup of West Germany, which was backed by NATO.

The dispute over Berlin now had to be weighed in the context of a full-fledged nuclear arms race. Eisenhower was averse to dramatic confrontations. The West German chancellor, Konrad Adenauer, pleaded with Eisenhower not to make any concessions to Moscow. Eisenhower believed that if the U.S. surrendered Berlin "then no one in the world could have any confidence in any pledge we make." But he also worried that the American commitment to the city could drag the U.S. into war. Berlin was "a can of worms," he confided to his son. He looked for ways to defuse tensions with Moscow, responding to Krushchev's ultimatum on Berlin with an invitation for the Soviet leader to visit the U.S. At their meeting at Camp David, Eisenhower agreed to participate in Four Power talks over the future of Berlin in exchange for Kruschchev's withdrawing his threats to force the West out of the city. It was a stopgap measure, but to Eisenhower the agreement represented progress. In his view, diplomacy, combined with steady resolve and patience, would prove to be the West's winning formula in the Cold War. The most realistic hope, he said, was "holding the line until the Soviets manage to educate their people. By so doing, they will sow the seeds of destruction of Communism as a virulent power."

Eisenhower strived to prevent the Berlin problem from overshadowing other priorities. The city returned to center stage under his successor. A young John Kennedy had toured Berlin after the Allied bombing campaign in 1945, and said "it will be many years before Berlin can clear the wreckage and get the material to rebuild." Some of Kennedy's aides believed that he needed to adopt a harder line against the Soviets: Kennedy should make it clear the United States would go to war to prevent Khrushchev from trying to force the Allies out of Berlin. As the historian Robert Dallek writes, "if there was to be a next world war, Berlin, Kennedy believed, would be where it began." Although Khrushchev was said to have "beamed with satisfaction" when told of Kennedy's election, the Soviet leader was also suspicious. He believed the young president was susceptible to pressure from "ruling circles" in the American establishment who were implacably hostile to the USSR. Khrushchev was determined to show Kennedy that the Soviet Union could not be intimidated.

Barely six months into his presidency, Kennedy met Khrushchev for a two-day summit in Vienna. The Kennedy administration had already suffered a humiliating setback, when a CIA plan to overthrow Fidel Castro, the communist leader of Cuba, met disaster at the Bay of Pigs. Khrushchev sought to exploit that American debacle and test the mettle of the young president. He believed Kennedy was weak. In Vienna, he repeated his demand that both superpowers sign a peace treaty with the East German government and that Western troops withdraw from Berlin. If the United States refused to recognize the GDR, Moscow would go ahead on its own and instruct the East Germans to cut off Western access to Berlin. Kennedy conceded that the Soviets could do what they wanted in

East Germany, but repeated the U.S. commitment to stay in Berlin. Khrushchev said, "it was up to the U.S. to decide whether there will be war or peace"; one way or the other the Soviets would move ahead with its plans in December. "Then it will be a cold winter," Kennedy replied.

The exchange with Khrushchev rattled Kennedy. "Worst thing in my life," Kennedy told James Reston of the *New York Times* in an interview after the summit. The Bay of Pigs fiasco, the president said, had convinced Khrushchev that "anyone who was so young and inexperienced as to get into that mess could be taken, and anyone who got into it, and didn't see it through, had no guts. So he just beat the hell out of me." Kennedy needed to regain his footing. Some of his advisers, including former Secretary of State Dean Acheson, pushed Kennedy to threaten Khrushchev with "the military option" if he made a move on Berlin and to prepare the country for the prospect of nuclear war. Kennedy wasn't so sure. He wanted to keep West Berlin under Western control, but he privately told his aides that saving East Berlin wasn't worth a war.

The Berlin crisis consumed the Kennedy White House. The president's brother, Robert, put the chances of war between the U.S. and the USSR at one in five. Kennedy's national security adviser, McGeorge Bundy, enlisted State Department counselor Abram Chayes and a brilliant young Harvard academic named Henry Kissinger to sketch out how a confrontation over Berlin would unfold; Chayes and Kissinger concluded that if hostilities broke out, there was little standing in the way of an all-out exchange of nuclear weapons.

The president asked two of his closest advisers, Ted Sorensen and Arthur Schlesinger, Jr., what a political solution would look like. They told him that Khrushchev was desperate to stop the flow of East Germans flooding into the West. Despite his bluster, Khrushchev feared a military conflict as much as Kennedy did. The president should find a way to project resolve but allow Khrushchev to save face. In a speech from the Oval Office on July 25, Kennedy announced that he would increase the U.S. defense budget and mobilize the reserves and build new weapons. He pledged the U.S. to defending the security and freedom of West Berlin, which had become "the great testing place of Western courage and will." He added that "our response to the Berlin crisis will not be merely military or negative. We do not intend to abandon our duty to mankind to seek a peaceful solution." Crucially, he repeatedly stressed the American commitment to *West* Berlin, which left it to the Soviets to do what they needed to do in the East. A few days later, he told his aide Walt Rostow that Khrushchev was "losing east Germany. . . . He cannot let that happen. He will have to do something to stop the flow of refugees—perhaps a wall."

Kennedy was right. East German leader Walter Ulbricht and his chief of security, Erich Honecker, had launched an operation to seal off the border between East and West Berlin with three hundred tons of barbed wire. They told Khrushchev of the plan in March 1961. Khrushchev initially rejected the idea, but soon came to see it as the best nonmilitary option for closing East Germany's borders. Still, he remained so nervous about it that he took a secret trip to inspect the proposed site of the barrier, traveling incognito and never getting out of his car. When he returned to Moscow, he gave the go-ahead to the plan but insisted that the Wall not encroach on West Berlin. Khrushchev fretted that Western troops might try to knock down the Wall before it was built.

Just after midnight on August 13, 1961, thousands of East German workers, soldiers, and police poured onto the streets of the darkened city to erect the barrier. By 6 A.M., the border between East and West Berlin was sealed. Though Berlin was full of spies, U.S. intelligence was caught by surprise. A West German journalist recalled watching barbed wire rolled out in front of the Brandenburg Gate and wondering why Western authorities failed to intervene. Crowds of bewildered, angry West Berliners gathered near the city's great monuments, yelling at the authorities and trying to help friends from the East crawl through the barbed wire. The East German regime soon deployed lines of troops with fixed bayonets to the border, followed by columns of tanks. Escape became nearly impossible. Subway lines that once linked the two sides of the city were halted before they entered West Berlin. East Berliners could be seen standing on balconies, helplessly waving handkerchiefs to neighbors in the West. On Bernauer Strasse, which straddled the borders, residents in apartment buildings that were part of the East began jumping out of their windows onto the street below, which was in the West. East German police raided buildings in the area, rounding up people before they tried to jump. Television footage showed one man sliding down the wall of a building as a crowd of West Berliners waited to catch him. Just then the police appeared in the window and began pulling him back up. The crowd grabbed his ankles and finally tugged him to the ground. He was free.

Kennedy received the news of the developments in Berlin at his family's compound in Hyannis Port, Massachusetts. When he returned to Washington, he gave the news a positive spin. The closing of the border showed that Khrushchev had been convinced not to try to seize Berlin by force. "It's not a very nice solution," he said, "but a wall is a hell of a lot better than a war." Kennedy viewed the outcome as a success. The communists had not attempted to shut off access to West Berlin from West Germany. "The other side panicked, not us," he said. "It's all over; they're not going to overrun Berlin."

What Kennedy misjudged was the impact of the Soviets' move on the morale of Berliners. Willy Brandt, the mayor of West Berlin, openly challenged the president to speak out against the Wall. "Berlin expects more than words," Brandt told a cheering crowd after the barrier went up. "Berlin expects political action!" Kennedy was stung. He announced plans to send 1,500 more troops to Berlin and dispatched his vice president, Lyndon B. Johnson, to the city, along with General Lucius Clay, the former governor of the American sector and architect of the Berlin Airlift, who would act as Kennedy's representative in Berlin. Johnson pleaded not to go. "They'll be a lot of shooting and I'll be in the middle of it. Why me?" he said. But once persuaded to accept the assignment, he carried it out with gusto. Hundreds of thousands of Berliners lined the streets as Johnson's motorcade carried him into the heart of the city. When he got out to walk part of the route, the crowds surged toward him. Johnson soaked it up, swigging from a local beer offered by one man and riding with the door of his limo open so that people could see him. By the time he left the city forty-eight hours later, his right arm was swollen from shaking so many hands. The goodwill offensive worked: after Johnson's visit, 63 percent of West Berliners said they were convinced of the American commitment to the city.

The erection of a barrier to keep them in made Berliners in the East more desperate to get out. Two weeks after the sealing of the border, two youths were killed by East German border police while trying to escape. Ulbricht and Honecker ordered the barbed wire removed and replaced by a structure made of concrete slabs. The barrier was now a wall. In late October, Clay set out to test the East Germans' willingness to allow American diplomats to cross into East Berlin, as they were legally permitted to do. On October 25, a car carrying a group of Americans attempted to pass through Checkpoint Charlie, a crossing point between the American and Soviet sectors. East German police stopped the car and questioned the diplomats. Clay ordered ten U.S. M-48 tanks outfitted with bulldozer fronts to the checkpoint, until the East Germans relented. Clay repeated the stunt the next day, but this time the Soviets responded, moving ten tanks into position opposite the American tanks at Checkpoint Charlie. It was the closest that American and Russian conventional forces ever came to direct confrontation in the Cold War.

Berlin was no longer simply a political problem between Washington and Moscow. It had the potential to spark a military conflict. Kennedy ordered his brother to tell the Soviet ambassador to Washington that the U.S. would pull back if the Soviets did. Twenty hours after it began, the standoff ended. Neither Khrushchev nor Kennedy wanted to go to war over Berlin.* But the divided city was an irresistible stage on which the contrasts between the superpowers could be drawn more starkly than anywhere in the world. "We have been handed a propaganda victory of tremendous dimensions on a silver platter," Robert Kennedy wrote to his brother after visiting Berlin in 1962. "And we are just not taking advantage of it."

In March 1963, the White House announced that the president would visit Berlin as part of a trip to West Germany, Italy, Great Britain, and Ireland. News of Kennedy's visit touched off such a rush of excitement in West Berlin that officials worried about the possibility that the crowds might try to take down the Wall. When Kennedy arrived in Berlin, at 10 A.M. on June 26, people greeted the motorcade as soon as it left Tegel Airport. Journalists reported that onlookers hung from trees, stood on flatbed trucks, and climbed to the roofs of gas stations to get a glimpse of the president. As Andreas Daum recounts in the book *Kennedy in Berlin*, the visit was choreographed by the West Germans, who wanted the Wall to be the visual focal point, as a way to highlight the encirclement of West Berlin. After Kennedy stopped at Checkpoint Charlie, an NBC correspondent reported that JFK had been "emotionally

---

* The Cuban missile crisis in 1962 spurred Khrushchev to reach out to Kennedy in an effort to avoid a nuclear confrontation. "Evil has brought some good," he wrote in one of a number of letters to the U.S. president. Kennedy did not make a full response to Khrushchev's overtures until June 1963, when he announced that he would send a representative to Moscow to begin talks on a nuclear test ban treaty. "We seek a relaxation of tensions without relaxing our guard," he said in a speech to the nation five months before his death. See Leffler, *For the Soul of Mankind*, pp. 158–191.

aroused by what he had seen"—though Kennedy later said he had been unable to get a clear glimpse of the Wall. At another stop, Kennedy stood on an observation deck that provided a view of the Wall and the Brandenburg Gate. The East Germans had hung curtains between the Gate's columns to prevent Kennedy from seeing the Unter den Linden.

Kennedy arrived at Berlin's Schöneberg City Hall shortly before 1 P.M. In Brandt's office just before taking the stage, he flipped through index cards that held the text of his prepared speech. On one of them he handwrote the words "Ish bin ein Bearleener"—his pronunciation of a phrase he had devised with McGeorge Bundy, his national security adviser, a week earlier. When he mounted the speaking platform above the Rudolph Wilde Platz, the president looked out on a crowd of some 500,000. He dispensed with his prepared remarks. "Two thousand years ago the proudest boast was civis Romanus sum. Today, in the world of freedom, the boast is ich bin ein Berliner." Kennedy waited for the remark to be translated before acknowledging the applause. In far stronger terms than he had done before, he condemned the Wall as "an offense against humanity" and "the most obvious and vivid demonstration of the failures of the communist system. . . . Freedom has many difficulties and democracy is not perfect, but we have never had to put a wall up to keep our people in." The crowd's energy gathered force as he closed. "All free men, wherever they may live, are citizens of Berlin," he said, "and therefore I take pride in the words: Ich bin ein Berliner." The translation of the last lines was drowned out by the crowd's chants of "Ken-NED-dy."

"We will never have another day like this one," the president told Sorensen aboard Air Force One. Kennedy was so taken by his reception in Berlin that he promised audiences that he would leave an envelope in the Oval Office for his successor. Inside, a note would read, "Go to Germany!" It is unlikely that he got around to fulfilling that promise in the remaining six months of his life.

Still, Daum writes that Kennedy's trip "was an event unparalleled in Germany's postwar history prior to the fall of the Berlin Wall in 1989." On the night of Kennedy's death, candles illuminated windows across West Berlin, a traditional German rite of mourning. At the Schöneberg City Hall, 250,000 people gathered in the square where Kennedy had spoken. Two American soldiers played taps. A representative speaking for Willy Brandt said of JFK, "He was a Berliner." Then the lights of the City Hall went out.

Berlin's significance to U.S. foreign policy faded after Kennedy's death. To most Americans, civil rights and the culture wars at home overshadowed the undulations of the U.S.-Soviet conflict. Mired in Vietnam, the Johnson administration looked for ways to broker a détente with the Soviets. The prospect of a confrontation over Berlin was one Johnson couldn't afford. Vietnam also turned West German public opinion against the United States. The German left increasingly viewed Washington and the pro-American government in Bonn—not the Soviets—as their biggest enemy. Even staunch German anti-communists like Willy Brandt began to advocate trade, exchange, and contacts across the divide between East and West Germany, rather than call for the divide to be eliminated altogether. The world learned to live with the Wall.

The East German regime became a notorious police state. The size of the East German secret police, the Stasi, tripled from 17,500 in 1957 to 52,700 by the early 1970s. The Stasi's peculiar genius was its ability to convince, or coerce, ordinary East Germans to inform on each other. Anywhere from 600,000 to two million East Germans worked for the Stasi during the forty-year existence of the GDR, out of a population of sixteen million. Even as standards of living improved from the depths of the postwar years—the number of East Germans who owned refrigerators rose from 6 percent to 54 percent in the decade after the Wall was built—political repression was an accepted fact of life. The Stasi rounded up tens of thousands of citizens on suspicion of subversion and political organizing. Some were sent to reeducation camps, the equivalent of the East German gulag. The luckier ones were deported to the West.

By the late 1960s, the Berlin Wall was a subject on the mind of only a small handful of American politicians. One was the governor of California. On May 15, 1967, Ronald Reagan agreed to a televised town hall debate with Robert Kennedy on "The Image of America and the Youth of the World." Kennedy and Reagan were both prospective presidential contenders. Aired on CBS from 10 to 11 P.M., the program attracted fifteen million viewers. The two men faced a panel of hostile international students, who mostly peppered them with accusations about U.S. misconduct in Vietnam. *Newsweek* gave Reagan credit for showing more command of "facts and quasifacts about the Vietnam conflict than anyone suspected he knew." But more revealing was an exchange with one student who asked Reagan whether the United States should normalize relations with governments like Mao Zedong's China. "The only objection that I've had with some of the building of bridges . . . is we haven't been hard-nosed enough," Reagan said. "When we signed the consular treaty with the Soviet Union, I think there were things we could have asked in return. I think it would be very admirable if the Berlin Wall . . . should disappear. I think this would be a step toward peace, toward self-determination of the peoples there." Reagan didn't want his opposition to the Wall to be mistaken for rash bellicosity. "We don't want the Berlin Wall knocked down so that it's easier to get at the throats of East Germans," he continued. "We just think that a wall that is put up to confine people, and keep them within their own country instead of allowing them the freedom of world travel, has to be somehow wrong."

The Wall offered Reagan a rhetorically potent symbol for his emerging critique of détente. In a speech in Miami on May 21, 1968, he advocated tying trade with the USSR to concessions in Berlin:

"If Russia needs our wheat to satisfy the hunger of her people, it might be well to point out that wheat could be delivered easier if there were no Berlin Wall between us." Even within his party, Reagan's suggestion that the United States pressure the Soviets to end the division of Berlin had few supporters. Shortly after taking office in 1969, President Richard Nixon made a three-hour visit to West Berlin. He was greeted by large crowds of West Berliners waving American flags, though protesters near the Kaiser Wilhelm Memorial Church also attempted to pelt his limo with eggs, carpet tacks, snowballs, and paint-filled bags. Nixon went to the border between East and West Berlin—now an obligatory stop for visiting dignitaries—and made a speech committing the United States to defend "the people of free Berlin." But he didn't mention the Wall.

Where once it had embodied the volatility of the early Cold War, Berlin and the wall running through it came to reflect the conflict's permanence. The Nixon administration's strategy of détente succeeded in improving relations between Washington and Moscow, but did little to offer hope for those trapped behind the Iron Curtain. In East Germany, the Stasi harassed, intimidated, and even jailed those who so much as applied for visas to travel to the West. The 1975 Helsinki Accords negotiated by the U.S. and Soviet Union ostensibly gave citizens throughout Europe "the right to free choice of place and residence." But for millions the Eastern Bloc remained a prison.

In 1978, one American visitor caught a glimpse of life on the other side of the Wall. When Reagan decided to run for president, two advisers from his gubernatorial days, Peter Hannaford and Richard Allen, organized two overseas trips to help him bolster his foreign policy credentials. His trip to Europe in November 1978 included stops in Paris and London, where he met with a rising Conservative Party star named Margaret Thatcher. In West Germany, the traveling party—which included Reagan's wife, Nancy, and Hannaford and Allen and their wives—stopped in Bonn, where Reagan met Helmut Schmidt, the chancellor, and Helmut Kohl, a young opposition leader. Reagan arrived in West Berlin on November 30, spending the night at the Kempinski Hotel. The next day the group got in two cars to drive into the Soviet sector. A representative of the U.S. consulate told them to keep their windows closed and not to hand their passports to the Soviet guards at Checkpoint Charlie. On the other side, they were struck by the desolation of the East. Buildings destroyed during World War II were still in ruins. They drove to the Alexanderplatz, the site of the biggest department store in East Berlin. While the women went inside, Reagan, Allen, and Hannaford stood on the edge of the square. They spotted two armed German police officers thirty feet away. Moments later the police accosted a man crossing the square and forced him to drop his bags and produce his internal passport. As the man searched for his documents, in Allen's account, one of the officers pointed the barrel of his machine gun at the man's chest.

As fleeting as it was, the incident stuck with Reagan, if mainly because it provided a handy scene he could use later to illustrate the inhumanity of communist rule. "Reagan thought this was a demonstration of repressive government in action," Hannaford says. "A citizen couldn't even walk across the plaza without being stopped by the police." Later that year Reagan twice made the plight of East German dissidents the subject of his daily radio broadcast, which was aired on 250 stations across the country. In a letter to a supporter sent on the eve of his 1980 presidential campaign, he lamented "the lost opportunity in Berlin when we could have knocked down and prevented the completion of the Wall with no hostilities following."

Reagan's indictments of the Soviet system were finding an audience. After the brief thaw of détente, East-West relations were entering another deep freeze. The USSR's growing assertiveness was highlighted by its deployment of SS-20 intermediate-range missiles in Eastern Europe. In October 1977, West German chancellor Helmut Schmidt publicly called on NATO to counter the Soviet threat by positioning its own missiles in Western Europe. The new American president, Jimmy Carter, had criticized Nixon, Ford, and their secretary of state, Henry Kissinger, for ignoring moral values and human rights in the name of maintaining the balance of power. And yet Carter did not initially want to provoke the leaders in the Kremlin. He wrote in his diary that "It's important that [Soviet leader Leonid Brezhnev] understand that the commitment I have to human rights first of all and that is not an antagonistic attitude of mine toward the Soviet Union."*

On July 15, 1978, Carter made the fourth presidential visit to West Berlin since World War II. He kept a lower profile than his predecessors, holding a town hall meeting with a handpicked audience of Berliners and stopping for a photo op at the Wall, which he later said "accurately reflects a wasteland of the human sprit." But if Carter had any faith in the West's capacity to alleviate such hopelessness in the Eastern Bloc, he didn't show it. When an elderly German woman asked him how long the Wall would stand, Carter responded, "I hope that it will be removed in the future, but I have no idea when it might be. I'm sorry, I can't give you a better answer, but that's the truth."

Carter's pessimism underscored the mood of a nation that, after Vietnam and Watergate, had lost confidence and belief in its authority on the world stage. Much of the world had resigned itself to the immutability of the Cold War. In 1963, when John Kennedy visited the U.S. military headquarters in West Berlin, he told the troops there that "no [U.S.] garrison served under comparable conditions, in territories surrounding it and with the adversar-

---

* Carter did not immediately deploy the missiles, but made arrangments to do so if arms control talks with the Soviets were not successful. In December 1979, ministers representing all fifteen NATO members unanimously approved the deployment of 572 Cruise and Pershing II missiles in Western Europe. The missiles were finally deployed in 1983.

ies so numerous." For three decades the U.S. used wise diplomacy and military steadiness to defend a city deep within its opponent's sphere of influence, without ever provoking an actual war. That was a remarkable achievement. And yet the division of Europe could not end so long as the Berlin Wall was standing. Who would take the initiative to tear it down?

No one knew the answer. If anything, the Soviets appeared even less open to persuasion. The Soviet invasion of Afghanistan on December 27, 1979, dashed any hopes that the Cold War might be winding down. Carter announced a boycott of the 1980 Olympic Games in Moscow and doubled the defense budget. He withdrew the SALT arms control treaty from consideration by the U.S. Senate. But it was too late to save his presidency. The storming of the U.S. embassy in Tehran and taking of sixty-six Americans hostages proved to be one humiliation too many. Reagan seized on the Carter administration's failures on the economy and foreign affairs, calling Carter's tenure "an American tragedy." Carter, in turn, cast Reagan as a reckless warmonger who lacked experience and judgment. Were it not for the lone presidential debate of the campaign, held on October 28, such doubts might have cost Reagan the election. But that debate reassured the public that the former governor was not a radical. Reagan clinched the presidency with his devastating closing statement: "It might be well if you ask yourself," Reagan said, looking straight into the cameras, "Are you better off than you were four years ago? . . . Do you feel that our security is as safe, that we're as strong as we were four years ago?"

One week later the voters delivered their answer. Reagan beat Carter by 10 percentage points and routed him in the Electoral College, 489–89. He took Carter's concession call at 5:35 P.M., as he stepped out of a shower at his room in the Century Plaza hotel in Los Angeles. After Reagan's victory speech, his supporters presented him with a cake shaped like the map of the U.S., with flags planted in the forty-four states Reagan had won. When the cake started to slide, Reagan quipped, "I thought maybe the world was going out as I was going in."

The new president took office at a time of public uncertainty about America's place in the world. Policymakers were divided about whether to placate or challenge a seemingly more assertive USSR. Most of all, the American people craved a leader who could restore the nation's self-belief at home and abroad. In *Time*'s report on the election, George J. Church wrote, "After four years of Jimmy Carter, Americans clearly yearned for someone who would do things differently." They got him.

2. THE LAST BEST HOPE

R onald Reagan was sworn in as the fortieth president of the United States on a balmy, 56-degree afternoon in Washington, one of the warmest inauguration days on record. The unseasonable weather seemed to fit the occasion, which commentators declared marked a new era in American politics. Reagan's victory would "usher in the Western conservatism that has been trying to break through for two decades," wrote the *New York Times* on the eve of the inauguration. To underscore the point, Reagan's team arranged for the ceremony to be staged for the first time ever on the west side of the Capitol, so that the new president could look out toward the American heartland. The night before the inaugural, he wrote the final version of his twenty-minute speech by hand on a yellow legal pad, inserting lines that previewed the themes of patriotic renewal that would come to define his presidency. "It is time for us to realize we are too great a nation to limit ourselves to small dreams," he said, adding, "I do not believe in a fate that will fall on us no matter what we do. I do believe in a fate that will fall on us if we do nothing." He responded to claims that the country faced "inevitable decline" with a classic Reaganism. "Those who say we are in a time when there are no heroes," he said, "just don't know where to look."

From the start, Reagan's presidency was touched with that indispensable ingredient to political success: luck. Carter had gone forty-eight hours without sleep leading up to the inauguration, hoping to secure the release of the hostages held in Tehran before he left office. Early on the morning of January 20, he received word that the hostages were on board planes at Tehran airport that would take them out of Iran. But the captors refused to let the planes take off until the afternoon, to deny Carter the chance to announce their release. Reagan was outraged by the Iranians' attempt to embarrass the outgoing president, but Carter insisted that nothing be mentioned until the hostages had left Iranian airspace. At 12:25 P.M., the moment Reagan began speaking, the planes rolled down the runway in Tehran. Carter left Washington for Plains, Georgia, immediately after Reagan's speech. At 2:15 P.M., the new president announced the release of the hostages at the traditional luncheon with congressional leaders. "The news seemed to turn the inauguration celebration, normally a highly festive occasion, into an event of unbridled joy," wrote Steve Weisman in the *New York Times*. That elation was most evident in the sixty-nine-year-old president himself. "It makes the whole day perfect," he said.

Reagan loved being president. He threw himself into the public performance of the presidency and left the details to his aides. "Surround yourself with the best people you can find, delegate authority and don't interfere as long as the policy you've decided is being carried out," he told one interviewer, describing his management philosophy. Reagan did not try to reinvent himself for the world's most important job; to a remarkable extent, he tailored the job to suit him. His aides devised a "script" of daily tasks that he could follow to a letter. His routine in the White House was so quotidian and predictable that he would cross off items on a to-do list as he completed them. After less than three weeks in office, he allowed an NBC News crew to follow him around, for a special called *Day in the Life of the President*. He was utterly unintimidated by the trappings of high office. After he left the White House he confided to one biographer, the journalist Lou Cannon, that "the biggest surprise at first was to find out how little surprise there was in the actual business of being President. . . . I was surprised at how unsurprised I was by the job. You just settled into it."

Reagan's even, unhurried temperament could be mystifying to those who worked for him, and led some to conclude he was detached from the job. He gave his aides few instructions about what he wanted them to do and rarely acknowledged or thanked them when they succeeded. His diary entries record social outings with an endless stream of associates from his California days, but most biographers have concluded that he had few confidants and that only his wife, Nancy, truly knew him. And for all his geniality, Reagan was stubborn. He refused to fire administration officials who got involved in scandals. He insisted on the truth as he saw it. A few days before the inaugural address, speechwriter Ken Khachigian removed a Reagan-devised anecdote about Martin Treptow, a World War I soldier who Reagan said was buried in Arlington National Cemetery. When Reagan asked why, Khachigian told Reagan that researchers assigned to the speech had found that Treptow was buried not in Arlington but in his hometown in Wisconsin. It didn't matter to Reagan. "Put it back in," he said.

That obstinacy could make it difficult to change Reagan's mind about someone or sway him from a policy position once he settled on it. "On things that mattered to him, the passive President could also be unyielding," Cannon wrote. To many of his conservative admirers, that resolve was essential to Reagan's greatness. By refusing to compromise his core principles, he conquered big government, stared down the Soviets, and won the Cold War. But the truth is that Reagan was more adaptable, politically shrewd, and open to compromise than either his champions or critics prefer to admit. He may have called the Soviet Union "an evil empire" but he was not above negotiating with it. He dramatically increased the U.S. defense budget and authorized fanciful new weapons programs, such as the "Star Wars" missile defense system, but he was sincere in his belief that such measures would convince the Soviets to give up the arms race and pursue peace. Where others saw the enmity between the superpowers as immutable, Reagan insisted that change was possible. In a dangerous and divided world, he allowed himself to dream that even the highest walls could one day fall.

Ronald Wilson Reagan was born in 1911, in Tampico, Illinois, a village of less than two thousand people. His mother, Nelle, was a seamstress who acted in local theater productions. His father, Jack, worked as a salesman at the local general store. Jack was a convivial Irish storyteller and an alcoholic. The family moved several times before Ron's tenth birthday, finally settling in Dixon, an industrial town twenty-five miles north of Tampico, with the Rock River running through it. One evening when he was eleven years old, Ron came home and found his father passed out in the snow in front of the family's home. Reagan dragged his father to bed. "I felt myself fill with grief for my father," he later recounted. He never mentioned the incident to his mother. Like many children of alcoholics, Reagan rarely spoke about how his father's addiction affected him.

The young Reagan sought escape by listening to the radio—which he first discovered by toying with a crystal radio set under a bridge in Dixon—and in books. "I was a voracious reader," he told his biographer. Among his favorite books were *Tom Sawyer, Huckleberry Finn*, and a religious novel called *That Printer of Udell's*, a fable about a poor son of an alcoholic who uses his power of oratory to become the moral leader of his Midwestern community. "I want to be like that man," Reagan told his mother.

As a teenager, Dutch—the nickname was given to him by his father, who said Ron looked like "a little Dutchman"—took a course in underwater lifesaving at the Dixon YMCA. He got a job as a lifeguard at Lowell Park, a beach set against a stretch of the Rock River. On August 3, 1928, the local newspaper reported that

Reagan had saved a man who was drowning in the river the night before; the paper said it was Dutch's twenty-fifth rescue, but his first publicly recorded one. Reagan felt he didn't receive enough credit from those he pulled out of the water—"People hate to be saved"—and so he began keeping his own record of rescues by making notches on a log. He thus recorded pulling seventy-seven people out of the waters of the Rock River. Reagan's experience as a lifeguard strengthened his self-belief and his conviction, instilled by his devoutly religious mother, that he had a special mission in life. "I've always believed in a divine plan and that God has such a plan for each one of us," Reagan later wrote.

Tall, handsome, and sturdily built, Dutch attended tiny Eureka College on an athletic scholarship, playing on the football team and washing the dishes at his fraternity to make extra money. His sense of humor and good looks made him popular with his peers; when students went on strike to protest budget cuts and call on the college president to resign, they nominated Reagan to speak at a rally in the chapel. Reagan remembered being given a "thunderous" ovation, which he found intoxicating. "I discovered that night that an audience has a feel to it, and in the parlance of the theater, that audience and I were together. . . . It was heady wine." Reagan soon took his first acting part, in a school production of an antiwar play called *Aria da Capo*. After college, Reagan was hired as a radio announcer at the local station in Davenport, Iowa. For his audition, he reconstructed from memory the fourth quarter of a Eureka football game, changing the ending so that he made the crucial block that led to the winning touchdown. The station moved to Des Moines and assigned Reagan to do play-by-play broadcasts of Chicago Cubs games. That involved describing the action based on a telegraph ticker that showed only whether a batter had made an out or a hit. The job helped Reagan develop the intimate, conversational speaking style that would endear him to the public. It also allowed him to indulge his capacious imagination. Once, when the telegraph broke down, Reagan had the batter foul off pitches repeatedly until the ticker was finally repaired.

Reagan's on-air persona made him a minor celebrity in the Midwest. He began giving speeches in the area, promoting temperance and healthy living to youth groups and civic associations. His ambitions broadened. On a trip to California with the Cubs in 1936, he scored a screen test with Warner Bros., who offered him a six-month contract to appear in movies. Reagan took it and convinced his parents to join him in California. The first of the fifty-three movies in which he appeared came out on June 13, 1937. The next year, he starred with the actress Jane Wyman in a movie called *Brother Rat*. The two began dating and married in 1940. Reagan's most famous roles came in the early 1940s. He played the dying Notre Dame halfback George Gipp in *Knute Rockne All-American*, and the trust fund heir Drake McHugh in *Kings Row*. But Reagan never became a true leading man (in *Knute Rockne*, he was on screen for just ten minutes) and as his acting career dimmed, he encountered personal setbacks. In May 1941, his father, Jack, died of a heart attack. With Wyman, Reagan had a daughter, Maureen, and a son, Michael, whom the couple adopted in 1945. But the couple's relationship was strained by the death of a third child, born four months premature, and by the divergence of their careers. They separated in 1948, the year Wyman won the Academy Award.

By then Reagan had found the stirrings of another passion. Like his father, who idolized FDR and once was employed by the Works Progress Administration, Reagan was a committed New Dealer. He did impressions of Roosevelt's fireside chats and memorized FDR's speeches, lines from which—"rendezvous with destiny," "arsenal of democracy"—he would later insert in his own. Plagued by poor eyesight, Reagan missed active duty in World War II. Instead he served as an officer in the Army Air Corps, directing, producing, and starring in films meant to prepare army fighter pilots for combat. He traveled the country speaking at parades and war bond rallies. By the end of the war, his views may have been "patriotic, idealistic and unformed," in Cannon's words, but his interest in politics had been awakened. He campaigned for Truman in 1948 and served as president of the Screen Actors Guild. As the historian Douglas Brinkley has written, Reagan adopted what he perceived to be FDR's worldview. "The world was divided into two camps: freedom versus totalitarianism." During the war, the totalitarian camp was embodied by Hitler's fascist regime. After the war freedom's enemy became communism and its chief proponent, the Soviet Union.

Reagan's views did not make him popular in Hollywood. His speeches to local groups denouncing Nazism were well received, but met with silence when he added warnings against communism. Reagan began to suspect communist subversion around him. At a meeting of a prominent Hollywood political committee on which he served, Reagan was shocked to hear one colleague harangue against the Truman administration's "imperialist" foreign policy and another declare that if the U.S. went to war with Russia, "I will be on the side of Russia." As the head of the actors union, he was forced to take sides in a labor strike by a new craftworkers union that leaned toward communism. When Reagan led the actors across the picket lines, the craftworkers responded with violence. An anonymous caller phoned Reagan on the set of a film and told him he would never be in movies again. Reagan would later cooperate with the FBI in its investigations into communist "influence" in Hollywood, but did not name names. Reagan wrote that "America faced no more insidious or evil threat than that of communism" but he was loath to demonize individual Americans for falling under its sway. Hollywood's liberals may have been misguided, but they were not malignant.

The defense of freedom was the central theme of Reagan's emerging worldview. In a speech to the all-female graduates at William Woods College in Fulton, Missouri, in 1952, he likened the war against Nazism to "the ideological struggle we find ourselves in today." He ended with a line that became a signature of the speeches that would catapult his political career. "With your help we can come much closer to realizing that this land of ours is the last best hope of man on earth," he said, for which the graduates gave him a standing ovation. Around the same time, Reagan's political allegiances started to shift. In 1952, he married Nancy Davis, a relatively unknown actress and stepdaughter of a wealthy Chicago conservative. In 1954, his movie career flagging, Reagan took a job with General Electric, as host of *General Electric Theater*, a popular weekly telecast. He also served as GE's traveling spokesman, visiting factories and plants across the country to bolster the company's image to its workers. By his own count, he visited 135 plants and met with 250,000 employees, making as many as fourteen appearances a day.

Reagan developed a stock speech that he delivered at luncheons, dinners, and banquets—what he termed "the mashed potato circuit." The speech emphasized the core tenets of Reagan's domestic philosophy: the keys to American prosperity were individual liberty, less intrusive government, and lower taxes. By elevating the state over the individual, communism was a direct affront to freedom and thus a threat to America's economic well-being. His speeches blended dense passages on economic and political thought with anecdotes, quips, and quotations from everyone from Karl Marx to James Madison. Whether or not he convinced audiences to embrace his brand of conservatism, Reagan convinced himself. "All these things I've been criticizing about government in my speeches . . . it just dawned on me that every four years when an election comes along I go out and support the people who are responsible for the things I'm criticizing," Reagan told his wife in 1958. He remained a registered Democrat, but by 1960, "I had completed the process of self-conversion."

Reagan's debut in Republican politics came in 1964. Though new to the party, he maneuvered to be elected California co-chairman of Barry Goldwater's presidential campaign. He continued to give versions of his mashed potato circuit speech—or simply, The Speech, as Reagan's admirers called it—to the GOP faithful in California. In late October, with the Goldwater campaign floundering, a group of supporters that included John Wayne gave the candidate a check for $60,000, which the Goldwater team used to buy airtime on national television. On October 27, Reagan appeared before a studio audience and addressed the nation. "I have been permitted to choose my own words and discuss my own ideas about the choice we face," he began. He launched into his by now crisply honed critique of taxes and regulation. Most indelible was the speech's conclusion, when Reagan blasted the idea of peaceful coexistence with the Soviet Union, calling it a "policy of accommodation" with the "most evil enemy mankind has known in his long climb from swamp to the stars. . . . We are being asked to buy our safety by selling into permanent slavery our fellow human beings enslaved behind the Iron Curtain."

Borrowing from his hero, FDR, Reagan finished by declaring, "You and I have a rendezvous with destiny. We can preserve for our children this, the last best hope of man on earth, or we can sentence them to take the first step into a thousand years of darkness." Later that night Reagan told Nancy, "I hope I haven't let Barry down." Instead, Goldwater's aides told Reagan that "A Time for Choosing," as the speech was also known, had brought in $8 million in donations—not enough to save Goldwater from a monumental defeat to Lyndon Johnson, but easily the campaign's biggest fund-raising event. Conservatives had found their standard-bearer.

Urged on by a group of wealthy activists, Reagan tested the waters of running for office. His speeches to Republican donors won him adulation he hadn't enjoyed since his Hollywood days. When he and Nancy appeared at a hotel in San Francisco, the line of well-wishers snaked around the block. In his book on Reagan's first gubernatorial campaign, *The Right Moment*, Matthew Dallek wrote that "Reagan continued to believe that a creeping tide of socialism threatened to overwhelm California and its forty-nine counterparts." By the summer of 1965 he decided to run for governor against the incumbent Democrat, Edmund "Pat" Brown. The state was in upheaval. Student protests convulsed the University of California and race riots broke out in Los Angeles. Reagan tapped into a public yearning for order. And yet Brown's advisers underestimated Reagan, believing his views were too radical for the electorate. One prominent Democratic fund-raiser, Manning J. Post, pleaded with Brown to take Reagan seriously. "This sonofabitch is going to beat the shit out of you. . . . You take an actor who had the image of a good guy; man, you can't overcome it. You just can't make him a bad guy anymore." He defeated Brown by one million votes, winning fifty-five of the state's fifty-eight counties.

As governor, Reagan cut public spending and shrank the state bureaucracy. He reformed welfare but also agreed to the largest tax hike in California's history. Though among conservatives he tended to his image as an ideological purist, Reagan worked closely behind the scenes with Democrats in the State Assembly. He learned to use his sense of humor to disarm his opponents. (Driving through one student protest at the University of California at Santa Cruz, Reagan was confronted by a young demonstrator who yelled, "We are the future!" Reagan scribbled a message on a piece of paper and held it up to the window. "I'll sell my bonds," it said.) Having never worked in an office, let alone held one, he showed little interest in the details of running the state, adopting the management style that he would carry into the White House. One close adviser, William Clark, developed a briefing system suited to Reagan's intellectual appetite: one-page "mini-memos" that simply listed the pros and cons of a given issue.

In 1968, Reagan made a late and ill-judged run for the Republican presidential nomination, losing to Richard Nixon. He returned to Sacramento and won a second term as governor in 1970. By the time he left office in 1975, he was far more popular than his party, whose image had been pummeled by Watergate and Nixon's resignation. Reagan trained his ambitions on the White House. He became a relentless critic of Gerald Ford's push for détente with the Soviets. Like other Cold Warriors of the time, Reagan denounced the Helsinki Accords, which obligated the Soviets to respect human rights in their country and in their East European satellites but also recognized the reality of communist control in Eastern and Central Europe.* Reagan and hard-liners like him charged that Ford had gone soft on the Soviets. "I am against it and I think all Americans should be against it," Reagan said. In late 1975 Reagan phoned Ford to tell him he was running for president.

Though he led in early polls, Reagan narrowly lost the New Hampshire primary and then the next five contests. Still, Ford did not clinch the nomination until the first roll call of delegates at the Republican National Convention in Kansas City. After accepting the nomination, Ford summoned Reagan to the floor. Reagan initially declined—"This is someone else's night," he said—but then made his way to the platform. He delivered an impromptu speech, thanking Ford and the delegates before conjuring an imagined future, about what it would be like to open a time capsule in a hundred years. "We live in a world in which the great powers have poised and aimed at each other . . . nuclear weapons that can in a matter of minutes . . . destroy, virtually, the civilized world we live in," he said. The people opening the time capsule would

---

* Drafted by the Conference on Security and Cooperation in Europe, the accords were nonbinding and aimed to enshrine respect for human rights and promote cooperation between East and West. The Ford administration was criticized by conservatives for signing the document, which also recognized the borders of communist-controlled Eastern Europe as permanent. But most scholars agree that the Helsinki Act helped create political space for many of the dissident movements in Eastern Europe that would ultimately end communist rule. See Wilentz, *The Age of Reagan*, pp. 58–59.

know whether a nuclear war had come about. "They will know whether we met out challenge," he said. "Will they look back and say, 'Thank God for those people . . . who headed off that loss of freedom, who kept us now 100 years free, who kept our world from nuclear destruction'?" When he finished, the crowd erupted with emotion. "Ronald Reagan could get a standing ovation in a graveyard," one delegate remarked.

From the moment he conceded defeat, Reagan started to look ahead. "Nancy and I, we're not going back and sit in a rocking chair and say, 'Well, that's all for us,'" he told his supporters. He urged them to "look at yourselves and realize there are millions of Americans out there who want it to be a shining city on a hill." After Ford lost the general election to Jimmy Carter, Reagan emerged as the front-runner for the GOP's nomination in 1980. He was no longer an insurgent; he had run twice and lost, and had not been elected to any public office in close to a decade. Reagan was nearing seventy. He shrugged off questions about his age—"There is nothing wrong with a little maturity," he quipped—but doubts resurfaced when he dropped the Iowa caucus to George H. W. Bush. He righted himself in New Hampshire with a trademark piece of political theater.

At the candidates' debate before the primary, Reagan, whose campaign was financing the telecast, had lobbied for other Republican hopefuls to be allowed to participate. Bush wanted to stick to the two-man format. After Reagan gave his introductory remarks, he attempted to introduce the other candidates on the stage, but the moderator cut him off. Reagan showed a rare flash of anger. "I paid for this show. I'm paying for this microphone, Mr. Green!" The line (lifted from a Spencer Tracy movie) drew roars from the audience; it reinforced his image as a no-nonsense tough guy. He regained momentum by winning the primary and, after sweeping the Southern states, earned the Republican nomination.

Reagan was evolving. He continued to view communism as repugnant and habitually referred to the Eastern Bloc countries as "captive nations." He criticized the SALT I and SALT II arms control treaties with Moscow. He insisted that he wasn't opposed to making deals with the Soviets, but didn't trust the Soviets to uphold them. And yet he felt that a war with Moscow was unthinkable. He believed that if the United States negotiated from strength, it could convince the Soviets to abandon the arms race altogether. "We should tell them we would be willing to sit at a long table as long as it took to negotiate a legitimate reduction of nuclear weapons on both sides," he wrote one supporter in July 1980, "to the point that neither country represented a threat to the other." On the plane back to Southern California after the Republican National Convention in Detroit, his political aide Stuart Spencer asked Reagan why he wanted to be president. "To end the Cold War," Reagan said. As related by former Secretary of the Air Force Thomas Reed, Reagan said the Soviet system was weak and would change if pressured to do so. He also expressed his fear of a nuclear war. "Reagan was not a hawk," Reed wrote in his memoir, *At the Abyss*. "He did not want to 'beat' the Soviets." As Reagan told Spencer, "There has to be a way, and it's time."

That desire to end the Cold War was alien to many of Reagan's allies on the right, who were more apt to view the USSR as an implacable, everlasting foe. After the Soviet invasion of Afghanistan, Carter's language hardened too. He called for reinstituting the draft and ordered an embargo on U.S. grain exports to Russia. Whatever he told his aides in private, Reagan couldn't afford to appear less hawkish than the man he was trying to replace. He ramped up his anti-Soviet rhetoric on the campaign trail and charged that Carter had been cowed by Moscow. With the economy sagging, the failed Desert One mission to rescue the Tehran hostages struck a further blow to the nation's morale. After the Republican convention, Reagan led by twenty-eight points.

Carter chipped away and by October the race was a dead heat. Polls showed that the public was inclined to like Reagan, but didn't know enough about him. After resisting a one-on-one debate with Carter for much of the campaign, Reagan's team reversed itself and the two men met on October 28, in Cleveland. Reagan's smooth, confident performance—"There you go again," he said in his most famous put-down—erased many of the doubts about him, while underscoring Carter's failures and lack of personal charisma. Among the 25 percent of voters who said they were undecided going into the last week of the campaign, Reagan won by an eight-point margin.

Reagan spent the transition at his home in Pacific Palisades, California. At the end of December, he was chosen as *Time*'s Man of the Year. For an interview with the magazine, Reagan wore a blue-and-green wool tartan jacket, a purple tie, white shirt, white hand-kerchief, black pants, and black loafers with gold trim. "In a lifetime one does not encounter half a dozen people so authentically at ease with themselves," concluded Roger Rosenblatt, the writer of the profile. "Reagan is a natural; he knows it. His intuitions are always in tune, and he trusts his own feelings."

At sixty-nine, Reagan was the oldest man ever elected president. By any standard he was extraordinarily robust for his age, six foot one inch tall and 185 pounds—as *Time* wrote, "the body of an actor . . . it has all but willed as tidy and organized an appearance as possible." His full, slicked black hair concealed a few slivers of gray at his temple. A naturally ruddy complexion made him appear on television as if he was wearing makeup, though he never did. Still, his body bore some of the tolls of age. In addition to his chronically poor eyesight, he was now nearly deaf in his right ear. Two years into his term, he became the first president to acknowledge being fitted with a hearing aid. And though he could recall anecdotes and recite from memory whole passages from books he read as a youth, he had trouble remembering the names of people he encountered on a daily basis. When confronted with questions about an issue he wasn't familiar with, he resorted to reading off index cards he kept in his breast pocket.

For a man of who had spent his entire adult life in the public eye, Reagan was a loner. He frequented Washington's social events but didn't attempt to make friends. He spent the equivalent of an entire year of his eight-year presidency at his ranch in the Santa Barbara Mountains. His pursuits were solitary: swimming, lifting weights, cutting brush, riding horses. "He doesn't let anybody get too close," his wife and closest confidante, Nancy, wrote in her memoir *My Turn*. "There are times when even I feel that barrier." That was most acutely evident in his relationships with his four children. Reagan didn't attend any high school football games played by his eldest son, Michael, a star quarterback in Arizona. Reagan's youngest son, Ron, was a dancer with the Joffrey Ballet; his parents never saw him perform. In his own way, Reagan acknowledged that his distance from the family was attributable in part to his own father's absence from his early life. "I don't know how to describe it because neither of my parents ever had anything in the line of formal education, and yet there was a freedom to make decisions," he said once, "and sometimes I find that maybe I go too far in that."

Reagan had few connections in Washington and relied on a small circle of aides from his gubernatorial years—in particular, Edwin Meese III and Michael Deaver—to manage his administration. The third member of the "troika" that ran the White House in the early days was James Baker, a fifty-year-old Houston lawyer who had been Bush's campaign manager, and was tapped to be chief of staff. With a recession looming, the new administration decided that domestic policy would take precedence over foreign affairs. One month into his presidency, Reagan addressed a joint session of Congress for the first time, unveiling a plan to slash eighty-three social programs, increase military spending, and reduce taxes by 30 percent over three years. He wrote the speech in longhand, on twenty sheets of legal paper, peppering it with road-tested exhortations and leaving blanks for the statistics his aides would fill in. "We're in control here. There's nothing wrong with America that we can't fix," he said. Reagan described the experience of addressing Congress as "a thrill and something I will long remember." If Americans remained unsure of the supply side economic theories behind Reagan's agenda, they instantly recognized in him a leader who could restore the nation's confidence. Polls taken after the speech showed that two-thirds approved of Reagan's approach to the economy.

On March 30, 1981, Reagan gave a speech to the national conference of the AFL-CIO at the Washington Hilton on Connecticut Avenue. He reminded the audience that he was a lifelong member of the AFL-CIO and made a pitch for his economic program. He finished the speech and walked out of the hotel at 2:25 P.M. As he raised his arm to wave to a crowd of onlookers, he heard a reporter shout "Mr. President!" Then came a crackling, popping sound. "What the hell's that?" he said to Secret Service agent Jerry Parr, who was already shoving the president into his limousine. Parr told the driver to head back to the White House. As the car sped away, Parr was lying on top of Reagan. "Jerry, get off. I think you've broken one of my ribs," Reagan said. Then he started coughing up blood. "Go to GW!" Parr shouted, realizing the president had been shot.

Three and a half minutes later the limousine arrived at George Washington University Hospital. Reagan was struggling to breathe but insisted on walking in. He collapsed just inside the entrance to the emergency room. "Getting shot hurts," Reagan later wrote in his diary. "No matter how hard I tried to breathe it seemed I was getting less & less air." And so he "focused on that tiled ceiling and prayed. But I realized I couldn't ask for God's help while at the same time I felt hatred for the mixed up young man who had shot me. . . . I began to pray for his soul and that he would find his way back to the fold." Nurses and paramedics stripped off the president's clothes; a breathing tube was inserted into his throat. His blood pressure plunged. Doctors inserted a catheter to drain blood from his lungs. "Doctors believe bleeding to death . . . 'Think we're going to lose him,'" the deputy press secretary, Larry Speakes, recorded in his notes. One hour after he arrived at the hospital, Reagan briefly regained consciousness. Doctors asked his permission to operate. "I hope you all are Republicans," he told the surgeons. As he was being wheeled into surgery, he saw Baker, Meese, and Deaver standing together in the hospital corridor. "Who's minding the store?" he joked.

The surgery lasted nearly three hours. Reagan had lost half his blood and had a collapsed lung. The .22 caliber bullet fired by the gunman, a twenty-six-year-old Texan named John Hinckley, Jr., had ricocheted off the presidential limousine and entered the left side of Reagan's body, above his rib cage. It stopped an inch from his heart. Through the night, Reagan slipped in and out of consciousness, scribbling notes because he was unable to talk. "Did they get the guy?" he wrote in one. "Where am I?" read a second. And another: "All in all, I'd rather be in Philadelphia," a quote from W. C. Fields. The next day he was informed that three others, including his press secretary, James Brady, had been shot. "Oh damn, oh damn," he said. He spent nearly two weeks in the hospital, fighting fevers and receiving heavy doses of intravenous pain medication. When he returned home on April 11, he was greeted by huge cheers from the entire White House staff, gathered on the South Lawn. Reagan, who lost twelve pounds in the hospital, went upstairs to the private residence and collapsed into a chair, but still found energy to write a long diary entry describing the events of the previous two weeks. "Whatever happens now I owe my life to God and will try to serve him in any way I can," he wrote.

The attempt on Reagan's life, and the courage he showed in surviving it, won him the admiration of many of his political adversaries. "The President has become a hero," the Democratic speaker of the house, Tip O'Neill, said, following Reagan's first public appearance, just one month after the shooting. Precisely how much the near-death experience changed Reagan is difficult to say, but it did reinforce his drive to fulfill what he saw as his God-given mission. "I have decided that whatever time I have left is for Him," he said. And so long as he was president, that meant continuing his crusade against the cruelty and repression of communist rule, while at the same time seeking to find a way out of the Cold War through personal diplomacy.

On April 18, 1981, one week after returning to the White House, Reagan sat in his private solarium and drafted, in longhand, a letter to the seventy-four-year-old Soviet leader, Leonid Brezhnev. Reagan had met Brezhnev in California in 1973, when Brezhnev came to the U.S. for a summit with Nixon. Brezhnev had sent Reagan a letter shortly after he took office, denouncing U.S. foreign policy and defending the Soviet invasion of Afghanistan. Now Reagan decided to write a response. He opened his letter by saying he understood "the somewhat intemperate tone of your recent letter. After all we approach the problems confronting us from opposite philosophical points of view." In gentle but insistent tones, he refuted Brezhnev's harangue against American "imperialism." After World War II, the United States followed a course "unique in all the history of mankind. We used our power and wealth to rebuild the war-ravaged economies of all the world including those nations who had been our enemies." Now, Reagan wrote, the U.S. and Soviet leaders had their own opportunity to save the world from the destruction of a nuclear war. "When we met I asked if you were aware that the hopes and aspirations of millions and millions . . . were dependent on the decisions that would be reached in your meetings. You took my hand in both of yours and assured me that you were aware of that and that you were dedicated with all your heart and mind to fulfilling those hopes and dreams."

To Reagan those dreams included "the dignity of [people]

having some control over their individual destiny. They want to work at the craft and trade of their own choosing and to be fairly rewarded . . . government exists for their convenience, not the other way around." He concluded the letter by informing Brezhnev that "in the spirit of helping the people of both of our nations," he intended to lift the grain embargo imposed by Carter. "Don't know whether I'll send it," Reagan wrote in his diary, "but I enjoyed putting some thoughts down on paper."

Reagan did send the letter, though he allowed the State Department to include a second, typed message conveying more traditional Cold War polemics. Brezhnev wrote back, "we are not seeking any standoff, and are making no attempt at your country's legitimate interests." But by emphasizing the differences between the two nations, Brezhnev seemed to rule out a personal dialogue with Reagan. In June Reagan made another attempt to reach out, asking that Brezhnev release Natan Sharansky, a Jewish dissident accused of spying for the U.S. "If you could find it in your heart to do this the matter would be strictly between us," he wrote, while avoiding further discussion of the issues separating the superpowers. "I agree with your observation that these matters are better discussed in person than in writing," he wrote. Again the overture met with Kremlin indifference, in part due to Brezhnev's poor health. But Reagan's desire to talk to the Soviets, and his unshakable confidence in his ability to persuade them to change their ways, was apparent. Anatoly Dobrynin, the Soviet ambassador to Washington, recalled that shortly after the assassination attempt, he was told by Paul Laxalt, the Nevada senator and longtime Reagan ally, about Reagan's letter to Brezhnev. Laxalt called it a "real psychological stride" for Reagan. He went on to say that Soviet leaders shouldn't be surprised if they were eventually to find in Reagan a partner in peace.

"Somewhere in the Kremlin," Reagan later wrote, "I thought, there had to be people who realized that the pair of us standing there like cowboys with guns pointed at each other's heads posed a lethal risk to the survival of the communist world as well as the free world."

As it turned out, there was at least one such leader in the Kremlin, but Reagan would have to wait for him to emerge. In the meantime, the American president—bloodied but unbowed—set out to change the world on his own.

3. ASH HEAP
OF HISTORY

I have a foreign policy; I'm working on it," the president wrote in a personal letter to journalist John Koehler in June 1981. Withstanding the assassination attempt and pushing through an economic program consumed the Reagan White House during its first year. Reagan made just one trip outside the United States, to Canada. Though Reagan privately pondered how to shape an approach to Moscow, in public he made few declarations of grand strategy. "I know I'm being criticized for not having made a great speech outlining what would be the Reagan foreign policy," Reagan wrote to Koehler. "I just don't think it's wise to always stand up and put in quotation marks in front of the world what your foreign policy is." Reagan was either spinning or deluding himself. For years, feuds among top administration officials produced a foreign policy that swung from hawkishness to conciliation. Reagan's diplomatic overtures to the Soviet leadership would be followed by covert initiatives to undermine it. Some of that incoherence was owed to the president himself, who initially gave mixed signals about how far he was willing to go toward confronting the Soviets. His position evolved as he learned on the job and conditions in the international scene changed. But his passivity and aversion to details—"You fellas figure it out," is how he concluded most meetings with his national-security team—left room for epic battles over who would define and control the Reagan message.

The administration was divided into two camps: pragmatists, who sought to moderate Reagan's rhetoric and broaden his appeal; and the true believers, loyalists who pushed for an uncompromising defense of conservative ideals. The pragmatists coalesced around the White House triumvirate of Baker, Meese, and Deaver. During the early days of the Reagan presidency, some hard-liners gravitated toward the National Security Council, which was run first by Richard Allen, a veteran of the Nixon and Ford administrations, and then William Clark, a strident anti-communist and one of Reagan's closest confidants. Clark's NSC sought to wrest control of the foreign policy agenda from the State Department. Reagan's first secretary of state, Alexander Haig, a blustery former NATO commander, lacked the trust of the president's top aides, who viewed him as reckless and impudent, particularly after he declared himself "in control here" in the hours after Reagan was shot. (Vice President Bush was flying back from Texas.) In one meeting, when the subject of Cuba's meddling in Central America came up, Haig said, "Give me the word and I'll make that island a fucking parking lot." Deaver later said he was horrified by Haig's militarism—"it scared the shit out of me"—and thereafter determined to prevent Haig from making appeals to the president's anti-communist zeal. Within a few months, he was plotting to force Haig out.

Deaver was the most powerful force in the molding of Reagan's public image. Fiercely loyal and tightly coiled, the forty-three-year-old Deaver saw himself as Reagan's protector, mapping out his daily schedule and controlling access to him. An aide to Reagan dating back to his gubernatorial days, Deaver held the title of deputy chief of staff, but his true talent was stagecraft: putting Reagan in visual settings that would capture the public imagination and emphasize the grand stature of the presidency. "Every morning after I get up I make believe I am him and ask what he should do and where he should go," he once said. If he rejected the hard-line anti-communism of the true believers—Deaver was wary of military adventurism and believed that the United States should pursue negotiations with the Soviets—he also recognized they could help to fashion Reagan's image as a bold, decisive leader. He knew how to produce the movie of the Reagan presidency. But he still needed someone to write the script.

The members of the White House speechwriting office considered themselves the truest believers of all. "By definition, we had to be closer to the president's way of thinking than anybody else on the staff," says Dana Rohrabacher, who worked in the White House for seven years. Another Reagan speechwriter, Clark Judge, says, "We all were very, very deeply versed in what the president's positions had been over the years, and we were there because of it. If you're in speechwriting, you carry a torch wherever you go." In the Reagan White House, the speechwriting office was populated by talented young wordsmiths drawn from the worlds of business, politics, and the media. With only a few exceptions, they were committed to the conservative cause and viewed Reagan in near-mythic terms.

The speechwriters learned from Reagan. It was not unusual for Reagan to rewrite drafts of speeches submitted to him, crossing out entire passages, removing words, and tightening language. Before delivering his speeches, he transcribed them into his shorthand on four-by-six index cards. He tinkered with the cadence and syntax of his speeches, almost always substituting a short, simple phrase for complex ones. Anecdotes, fables, sentiment, and humor were essential. "He had about thirteen rules of thumb," Rohrabacher says. "Not to use polysyllabic words and make sure it can be easily translated; not to go on forever and make sure you don't have a speech for more than half an hour. Make sure you always start out with a little funny story. And make sure there's a little inspirational story at the end. And maybe one little funny thing in the middle."

Reagan's first speeches as president, including the inaugural address, were drafted by Ken Khachigian, who had worked in the Nixon White House. Before moving to Washington, Khachigian had told Reagan he did not intend to stay in the job longer than six months. When he left, his duties were assumed by a thirty-one-year-old writer named Anthony Dolan. A Yale graduate, Dolan had been raised by Democrats but believed the party had gone soft on communism. After college he became a newspaper reporter and won a Pulitzer Prize for an exposé on government corruption in Stamford, Connecticut. Dolan was known for wearing cowboy boots to work and smoking cigars in his office in the Old Executive Office Building. He possessed an encyclopedic knowledge of Reagan's speeches, having begun studying them when he was thirteen.

When it came to speeches dealing with the Cold War, the speechwriters found themselves in regular conflict with the moderates in the White House, the National Security Council, and State Department. At the same time, those closest to Reagan knew the significance he attached to his public performances, and were sympathetic to the speechwriters' belief that their lines would resonate once Reagan delivered them. "If we're going to govern in bold colors, as he said, his writers shouldn't be composed in plaid," wrote David Gergen, the communications director. The trappings of the modern presidency—the permanent, traveling press corps, and the emergence of twenty-four-hour cable news—meant that every presidential address was now instantly available to millions around the planet. For Reagan, as much as for any president before or since, speeches were indispensable to the world's understanding of his core beliefs. To Dolan and his fellow writers, each speech constituted a defining moment. They were determined that Reagan seize it.

Reagan's first major overseas trip took place in June 1982, when he visited France, the Vatican, Italy, Britain, and West Germany in the span of eight days. Deaver had planned the itinerary for almost a year, focusing on backdrops and photo opportunities; he was most taken with the idea of Reagan's riding horseback with Queen Elizabeth at Windsor Castle. "Carter couldn't have done a thing like that," he told one British official. Dolan, meanwhile, focused on the president's June 8 speech to a joint session of Britain's Parliament, the first ever by a U.S. president. Dolan had been marginalized by the pragmatists in the White House, but his ambition was undimmed. On his own, he wrote up a twenty-three-page draft, steeped in references to history and philosophy, which condemned the "evil" character of the Soviet regime, "a militaristic empire whose ideology justifies any . . . violence if done in the name of the state." But he also emphasized the dysfunction of the Soviet system and predicted it would end up on "the ash heap of history."

Reagan, who had already rejected drafts of the speech submitted by the NSC, lit up when Clark gave him a copy of Dolan's draft. His attitude toward Moscow had hardened after the failure of his personal overtures to Brezhnev and the communist crackdown on striking shipworkers in Poland. The president made extensive revisions to Dolan's draft, excising long quotations and condensing other passages. He removed Dolan's references to the USSR as evil. He inserted four of his own handwritten pages. "There will be other Polands and we have known there are those who struggle and suffer for freedom within the confines of the Soviet system itself," he wrote. "How we conduct ourselves here in the western democracies will determine whether this trend continues." Even as he warned against "the march of those who seek disruption and conflict throughout the world . . . [an] assault on the human spirit called Marxism-Leninism," he also borrowed from Winston Churchill to stress that conflict was not inevitable, a theme he returned to throughout his life. "Our fortunes are still in our own hands and we hold the power to save the future," he wrote.

Reagan delivered the speech in the cavernous, high-ceilinged hall of the Royal Gallery. It was boycotted by 195 of 225 MPs from the Labour Party and met with applause just once, when Reagan paid tribute to British troops fighting in the Falklands. The Kremlin charged that the speech "may risk global catastrophe." But it thrilled British prime minister Margaret Thatcher, who nodded approvingly from the front row. In soaring if still relatively general language, the speech highlighted Reagan's faith in democracy and conviction that communism was doomed. And like his more famous address at the Brandenburg Gate five years later, the Westminster speech proved Reagan (and Dolan) prescient. Its passages about the economic decay of the Soviet system—Moscow faced "a revolutionary crisis," Reagan said—echoed the assessments of some Russian analysts. A few weeks earlier in Moscow, a young agriculture official had presented the Politburo with a plan to reform the country's moribund rural sector; without major changes, he warned, the Russian people would no longer be able to feed themselves. "Is it really that bad?" Brezhnev had asked.

The Westminster address and Dolan's dogged insistence on getting his draft to the president earned Dolan the adulation and loyalty of his colleagues. The speech became a template for their future statements on the Cold War. "The Westminster address presented Reagan's point of view; it grounded it in historical understanding," says Peter Robinson, whom Dolan would assign to write Reagan's 1987 speech in West Berlin. "Major Reagan speeches covered a lot of ground. . . . If you were to ask, what influences do you suspect were at work in your own mind as you drafted this? I would certainly say: the Westminster address." Dolan, Robinson says, "was a great champion of content. Tony would always argue: 'Give him a narrative; include history; include the argument.'"

Reagan's next stop on the European trip was West Germany, which he had first visited three years earlier. U.S. diplomats in Germany had pushed for Reagan to stop in Berlin. "The President's presence in Berlin would emphasize in a dramatic way the commitment of the U.S. to the freedom and security of Berlin," wrote Arthur Burns, the U.S. ambassador, in a March cable to Washington. "I would anticipate an outpouring of sympathy from the majority of Berliners who realize that American determination and the President's personal courage are the only true guarantors of Berlin's security and freedom." This was not a hard sell to Reagan's team, which had already identified the Berlin Wall as a target in their efforts to highlight repression in the communist world. Reagan had sent a message to the people of West Berlin in September 1981, on the twentieth anniversary of the Wall's construction. The mayor of the city, Richard von Weizsäcker, wrote back, "We hope with you, Mr. President, that the day will come when the Wall will not split Berlin any longer." Reagan also invoked the Wall during the Westminster speech, calling it a "symbol of power untamed" a "dreadful gray gash" and "the signature of the regime that built it."

The stop in West Berlin lasted just a few hours. Reagan had come from Bonn, where he addressed the German Bundestag. He said he was committed to counter Moscow's deployment of SS-20 missiles in Europe, but also acknowledged the fears of anti-nuclear protesters who had greeted his arrival with raucous demonstrations. "For those who march for peace, my heart is with you," he said. When a heckler twice yelled "What about El Salvador?" during Reagan's speech, he looked up and said, "Is there an echo in here?" The audience laughed and applauded. His speeches in Berlin were written by Landon Parvin, a former comedy writer and one of the few moderates in the speechwriting office, and Aram Bakshian, a fluent writer who had worked for Nixon and Ford. "I would be assigned things where they wanted something not as strident, but more peaceful," says Parvin. "We were trying to strike a fine balance between calling the Soviet Union for what it was but by the same token trying to reassure people."

In Berlin, Parvin said, Reagan was "focused on reassuring the German people he wasn't a cowboy." Speaking to twenty thousand people at the Charlottenburg Palace, Reagan's tone was more measured than it had been in London. "Ours is a defensive measure. We pose no threat to those who live on the other side of the Wall." He invited the Soviets "to reduce the human barriers—barriers as bleak and brutal as the Berlin Wall itself—which divide Europe." Reagan, nearing the end of the ten-day trip, was visibly exhausted. But being on stage revived him. When he spoke to a throng of U.S. troops at Tempelhof Airport, the staging point for the Berlin Airlift, he said, "I'd like to ask the Soviet leaders one question. In fact, I may stuff the question in a bottle and throw it over the Wall when I go there today. I really want to hear their explanation. Why is that Wall there?" At the end of his remarks, he ad-libbed one of his favorite anecdotes, about a World War II pilot who died with the gunner of his B-17 bomber when the plane was hit. "Never mind, son, we'll ride it down together," were the pilot's last words, according to Reagan, who said the captain was later awarded the Congressional Medal of Honor. In contrast, the Soviets had recently given an award to the murderer of Leon Trotsky. "I don't know of anything that explains the difference between the society we're trying to preserve and the society we're defending the world against than that particular story," he said. At that, the troops erupted in cheers. It didn't matter to Reagan that the tale of the B-17 pilot was almost certainly fictitious, so long as the audience ate it up.

Like his presidential predecessors—Kennedy, Nixon, and Carter—Reagan made a stop at the Berlin Wall. At Checkpoint Charlie, he got out of his limousine and walked over to the white line separating the U.S. and Soviet zones. He dangled his foot over the white line, into Soviet territory, then pulled it back and laughed. A reporter asked what he thought of the Wall. "It's as ugly as the idea behind it," he said. When another journalist asked if he believed Berlin would one day be united again, Reagan answered, "Yes."

•   •   •

Reagan's trip concluded without any moments comparable to the dramatic declaration he would make on his next visit to the city, five years later. In the summer of 1982, there was little sign that tangible change was coming in Eastern Europe, or that relations between Washington and Moscow would soon improve. On November 10, Reagan received word that Brezhnev had died. He declined to attend the funeral in Moscow, instead going with Nancy to sign a condolence book at the Soviet embassy in Washington. "There's a strange feeling to that place," Reagan wrote in his diary. "No one smiles." Brezhnev's successor, Yuri Andropov, the former head of the KGB, was a calculating, humorless technocrat. George Shultz, who had replaced Haig as secretary of state and met Andropov at Brezhnev's funeral, thought the new Soviet leader possessed "a capacity for brutality."

Shultz had served as secretary of labor and secretary of the treasury in the Nixon administration and had become friendly with Reagan after the former governor left Sacramento. Shultz had played football at Princeton and brought to the job a lugubrious stoicism that earned him respect, if not affection, among the president's advisers. Like Reagan, Shultz believed that the United States should counter Soviet influence by rebuilding the military and promoting democracy and open markets around the world. He also believed that the U.S. should negotiate with Moscow to reduce Cold War tensions, even if that meant dealing with unattractive leaders like Andropov. From the start of his tenure, Shultz lobbied for personal access to Reagan and pushed the president to talk with the Soviets. "Almost forgot—Geo. Shultz sneaked Ambassador Dobrynin (Soviet) into the White House," Reagan wrote in his diary on February 15, 1983. "We talked for 2 hours. Sometimes we got pretty nose to nose." Reagan told Dobrynin that he wanted Shultz to deal directly with Andropov, "no bureaucracy involved." Dobrynin told Shultz that "this could be an historic moment."

But Reagan wasn't yet ready to lay down his rhetorical swords.

While Shultz was secretly smuggling the Soviet ambassador into the Oval Office, Dolan worked on a draft of a speech the president was to deliver to the National Association of Evangelicals in Orlando, Florida. Most of the speech dealt with social issues like school prayer and abortion. The final third was devoted to foreign policy and to a scathing, moralistic attack on the Soviet Union. Dolan borrowed lines discarded from the Westminster speech: the Soviets were "the focus of evil in the modern world"; those who blamed both sides for the Cold War ignored "the aggressive impulses of an evil empire." Because it was not officially a foreign policy speech, it was not widely distributed at the State Department, which would have reeled at such language. Pragmatists in the West Wing, including National Security Adviser Robert (Bud) McFarlane, did send the speech back with the "Evil Empire" passage crossed out. The speechwriters managed to get a draft with much of the original language restored directly to Reagan, who made changes in the section on domestic policy but didn't touch Dolan's passage on the Soviets. The speech was a bombshell. The *New York Times* played it on the front page: "Reagan Denounces Ideology of Soviets as 'Focus of Evil,'" the headline read. Reporters asked White House aides what Reagan thought he could accomplish with such inflammatory talk. "The President knows what he is doing with his speeches," Gergen said.

Shultz was furious that the "Evil Empire" speech had been given without his consent. But there was more to come. Two weeks later, Reagan addressed the nation from the Oval Office to discuss his plans to strengthen the national defense. For years he had been intoxicated with the idea of a defensive shield that could protect the United States and its allies from a nuclear attack; if a true defense against such weapons existed, he believed, the world would never have to fear a nuclear Armageddon. Reagan found abominable the notion that the only thing standing in the way of war between the superpowers was their mutually assured destruction if a nuclear exchange took place. "What if free people could live secure in the knowledge that their security did not rest upon the threat of instant U.S. retaliation to deter a Soviet attack?" With that in mind, he wrote out by hand a new ending to his March 22 speech, calling for a "long-term research and development program" aimed at achieving "our ultimate goal of eliminating the threat posed by strategic nuclear missiles."

Another diplomatic uproar ensued. Democrats scoffed at the exorbitant cost of the president's Strategic Defense Initiative. Scientists dismissed the idea that a missile shield would actually work. Moscow charged that Reagan was abandoning the traditional theory of nuclear deterrence—which, of course, he was. "This is insane," Andropov said. Even Reagan's advisers were skeptical. "I understand the moral ground you want to stake out," Shultz told Reagan, but the technology wasn't advanced enough. Privately Shultz called the idea "lunacy." It didn't bother Reagan. "I felt good," he wrote in his diary the night of the speech. For Reagan, the idea of missile defense was never intended to be as destabilizing as the Soviets and some of his advisers feared. If a reliable shield could be built, he would share the technology with Moscow.

Reagan continued to alternate between talking tough and making gestures of conciliation. He had proposed that both sides eliminate their intermediate-range missiles in Europe—known as the "zero-zero" option—but when Moscow refused, he ordered Pershing missiles sent to Britain and West Germany. He stepped up support to anti-communist rebels in Nicaragua and Afghanistan. Still, he wrote to Andropov that "You and I share an enormous responsibility but to do so will require a more active level of exchange than we have heretofore been able to establish. . . . If you wish to engage in such communication you will find me ready." In the fall, a U.S. exercise designed to test command and control procedures in the event of a nuclear exchange caused panic in the Kremlin, which believed the United States was preparing a first strike. Soviet war-

planes were put on combat alert. The false alarm left Reagan genu-
inely shaken. "The Soviets are so . . . paranoid about being attacked
that without being in any way soft on them, we ought to tell them
no one here has any intention of doing anything like that." In a
speech in Japan shortly after the scare he declared, "A nuclear war
can never be won and must never be fought."

Prodded by Shultz and McFarlane, the White House began
to soften its public statements toward Moscow. The true believers in the speechwriting office found themselves squeezed out, no
longer allowed to meet with the president each week. In January
1984 Reagan again spoke from the Oval Office and made his most
conciliatory remarks to date. "The fact that neither of us likes the
other system is no reason to refuse to talk," he said. Gone was the
abrasive and confrontational tone of Dolan's "Evil Empire" speech.
"We want more than deterrence. We want genuine cooperation.
We seek progress for peace. Cooperation begins with communication." The speech concluded with a treacly anecdote Reagan had
penned in longhand, in which he imagined a meeting between two
Russians named Ivan and Anya and two Americans named Jim and
Sally. "Would they debate the differences between their respective governments? Or would they find themselves comparing notes
about their children and what each other did for a living?" Perhaps, Reagan said, they might even decide "that they were all going
to have dinner sometime soon." Though the Kremlin openly ridi-
culed Reagan's sentiment, Shultz met a few days later with Foreign
Minister Andrei Gromyko, at which the two men agreed to resume
negotiations. "The ice was cracked," Shultz said.

Reagan's more soothing tone fit the national mood of optimism.
Inflation had fallen by more than 9 percent, unemployment was
low, and the economy was growing at a robust 7.2 percent. "America is back," Reagan said triumphantly as he launched his bid for
reelection. The president's handlers set out to find ways to cap-
italize on the new surge of patriotism. The fortieth anniversary

of D-Day was June 6, 1984, and Deaver had decided that Reagan should go to Europe to mark the occasion. With his special assistant, William Henkel, Deaver visited the sites where the U.S. Army had gone ashore during World War II. As historian Douglas Brinkley recounted, Deaver and Henkel walked the nine-mile stretch of the Normandy shoreline that encompassed Utah Beach and Omaha Beach. They stopped at a windswept promontory overlooking the English Channel, known as Pointe du Hoc. A granite monument paying homage to the men of the U.S. Army 2nd Ranger Battalion, who withstood enemy fire to scale the cliffs there, was to be unveiled on the anniversary. Deaver had found his spot. He envisioned footage of Reagan's speech being replayed at the Republican National Convention. "I knew it would be our backdrop for the year," he later said.

Reagan was to give two speeches on D-Day. The new head of the speechwriting office, Ben Elliott, tapped Dolan to write the longer policy-focused address, which Reagan would deliver at Omaha Beach. The remarks at Pointe du Hoc were assigned to a thirty-three-year-old newcomer named Peggy Noonan. Born in Brooklyn, Noonan was the first member of her family to attend college. She had drifted toward conservatism during Vietnam, put off by the anti-American excesses of the far left. After college she got a job at CBS, eventually writing radio commentaries for Dan Rather before Elliott summoned her to the White House. Noonan spent hours reading bound volumes of presidential speeches dating back to George Washington. She developed a particular affinity for the ringing, rhythmic oratory of FDR. "This is how Reagan should sound," she told herself.

Noonan got to the office late, read the papers, watched Phil Donahue, called friends, and traded gossip. After lunch and a nap, she started to write, working late into the night with coffee and cigarettes nearby. Pointe du Hoc "was my first really big speech and I really wanted it to be good." After she had gone through a half-dozen drafts, she was told by the White House advance team that sixty-two members of the 2nd Ranger Battalion would be in attendance when Reagan delivered the speech. So she started over. Finally, on her fifteenth draft, she sent the speech to Elliott. She had borrowed both from the World War I poet Stephen Spender and from a recent book on the Brooklyn Dodgers, *The Boys of Summer.*

Reagan's entourage arrived in Normandy aboard the Marine One helicopter just after 1 P.M. on June 6. He went first to Pointe du Hoc. The sky was overcast and a brisk breeze made the flags snap. Though the edited version of the speech was to last just eight minutes, Deaver ensured that the network television correspondents traveling with Reagan played it as a major presidential address. It aired live on the morning news shows in the States. Reagan recounted the story of the soldiers who had fought there four decades earlier, then turned to the veterans seated before him. "These are the boys of Pointe du Hoc," he said. "These are the men who took the cliffs. These are the champions who helped free a continent. These are the heroes who helped end the war." When it was over, most of the audience was in tears. By the time he gave his second speech, at Omaha Beach, so was Reagan.

Though remembered for its soaring tribute to World War II heroism, the Pointe du Hoc speech also contained elements of Reagan's familiar anti-communist rhetoric, while again reiterating his desire to find a peaceful end to the Cold War. "We look for some sign from the Soviet Union that they are willing to move forward . . . there must be a changing there that will allow us to turn our hope into action. We will pray forever that some day changing will come." Privately, Reagan had begun an exchange of letters with Konstantin Chernenko, a former aide to Brezhnev who became general secretary after Andropov's death in February 1984. Reagan wrote in his diary that he wanted to meet with Chernenko "man to man," though no summit between the leaders ever came about. Chernenko contracted pneumonia in the summer and by the fall was unable to walk. The Kremlin instead dispatched Foreign Secretary Gromyko to meet with Reagan at the White House. Reagan found him "hard as granite." But in a moment Reagan recounted in his memoirs, Gromyko took Nancy Reagan aside and asked her, "Does your husband believe in 'peace'?" Nancy said yes. "Then whisper 'peace' in your husband's ear every night," Gromyko said.

Support for Reagan's foreign policy initiatives was far from universal. The U.S.'s intervention in Lebanon had ended in disaster, when a suicide bomber blew up the U.S. Marine barracks in Beirut, killing 241 servicemen. The administration's obsession with arming the contras in Nicaragua provoked a backlash on Capitol Hill and would soon sow the seeds of a crippling scandal. Its huge increases in defense spending were lambasted both by liberals and small-government conservatives. But Reagan's emphasis on promoting freedom and negotiating from strength sat well with the American people, as did the booming economy and the burst of national pride that came out of the 1984 Olympics in Los Angeles. "It's morning again in America," intoned Reagan's campaign ads as he headed into the general election against Walter Mondale. Reagan stumbled badly in the first presidential debate, appearing confused and unsure about the details of his own policies. "I didn't feel good about myself," he wrote in his diary. In the second debate, Reagan employed one of his trademarks: faced with doubts, he turned them into a laugh line. "I will not make age an issue in this campaign. I'm not going to exploit, for political purposes, my opponent's youth and inexperience," he said. The performance turned a close race into a rout. On election day, Reagan won 59 percent of the popular vote. He carried every state but Minnesota, Mondale's home state.

With a second term secured, Shultz, with Reagan's backing, stepped up his efforts to begin talks with the Soviets. Reagan told the secretary he wanted the "total elimination of nuclear weapons" to be the goal of negotiations, an idea he repeated in his second inaugural speech. "We are not just discussing limits on a further increase of nuclear weapons. We seek, instead, to reduce their number. We seek the total elimination one day of nuclear weapons from the face of the Earth." Reagan also extolled his pet project, the Strategic Defense Initiative, which he said would "render nuclear weapons obsolete."

The start of the second term occasioned shuffling in the White House. Baker, the chief of staff, traded jobs with Treasury Secretary Donald Regan, a blunt, short-tempered former Merrill Lynch executive. Regan loathed the speechwriting office, which he felt had gained too much influence. He immediately cut off the speechwriters' access to the president. Deaver, the impresario who had staged Reagan's most memorable public performances and who appreciated the importance the president attached to his speeches, soon left the White House.

The more momentous changes took place not in Washington but in the Kremlin. Chernenko's health deteriorated in the spring of 1985. He was suffering from emphysema, hepatitis, and cirrhosis of the liver. On March 10, he succumbed to heart failure, the third Soviet leader to die in less than two years. Upon hearing the news, the seventy-four-year-old Reagan told Nancy, "How can I be expected to make peace with them if they keep dying on me?" The next day, the Politburo elected a gregarious, self-assured, fifty-four-year-old government minister, the same man who years earlier had warned Brezhnev of the impending collapse of the Russian economy, to be the new leader of the Soviet Union. His name was Mikhail Gorbachev.

4. FIRESIDE TALKS

On the night of Chernenko's death, Gorbachev went for a walk in the garden of his country house outside Moscow. Snow lay on the ground, and it was nearly dawn. "We just can't go on like this," he told his wife, Raisa. Gorbachev had been preparing for the moment for years. He was groomed for leadership by Yuri Andropov, the former head of the KGB who became general secretary in 1983. Andropov tapped Gorbachev to oversee the reform of the Soviet economy. "Act as if you had to shoulder all the responsibility one day," Andropov told him. After Andropov's death, Gorbachev became the acting head of state, running most meetings of the Politburo, since Andropov's successor, Chernenko, was often too sick to attend. To Gorbachev, the morbid succession of infirm Soviet leaders was an apt metaphor for the rot eating away at his country's soul. "The system was dying away," he later wrote. He believed it was his mission to save it.

Doing so, Gorbachev told his comrades, would require dramatic steps: modernize the Soviet economy, promote competition, stamp out corruption, and make the political system more transparent. Gorbachev was a committed socialist and patriot, who admired the early Soviet leaders' success at lifting millions out of poverty and illiteracy. The Russian people had access to basic services, such as health care, and there was less social polarization than in the West.

And yet the country's stagnancy depressed him. In his travels to Western Europe, Gorbachev came to the conclusion that "people lived in better conditions and were better off than in our country." The rivalry with the United States had distracted Russian leaders from the job of improving the living standards at home. Military spending accounted for a full 20 percent of the country's GDP. To rescue itself from economic ruin, the USSR needed to find a way out of the Cold War. Gorbachev and his closest advisers knew this. "We want to stop and not to continue the arms race," he said in accepting his appointment as general secretary on March 11, 1985.

Gorbachev grew up in Privolnoye, a village in the southern Russian region of Stavropol. His grandfathers were peasant farmers who both ran afoul of the Communist Party and spent time in Stalin's concentration camps. Life in Privolnoye was primitive. The village consisted of "adobe huts with an earthen floor, and no beds at all"; sleeping involved lying on top of a stove and using rags as cover. In the early 1930s, famine devastated Privolnoye. One-third of the villagers died of hunger, including three of his father's siblings. When Gorbachev was ten, Germany invaded Russia, and Gorbachev's father and all other men in the village were conscripted to fight. The village fell to the Nazis in August 1942. Until the Red Army retook Privolnoye in January 1943, Mikhail lived in fear that his family would be executed.

His experiences during the war haunted Gorbachev. The family was told that Mikhail's father had died on the front, only to receive a letter from him four days later assuring them he was alive. Even more searing was the winter afternoon when Mikhail stumbled upon the remains of Red Army soldiers killed in a forest on the outskirts of town. "It was an unspeakable horror," he recalled. "Decaying corpses, partly devoured by animals, skulls in rusted helmets, bleached bones . . . there they lay, staring at us out of black, gaping eye-sockets." To Gorbachev's generation, the war "burned us, leaving its mark both on our characters and on our view of the world."

The young Gorbachev was resilient and ambitious. He worked diligently to make up the two years of school lost to the war. He excelled as a student and became a leader of the Young Communist League. His peers remembered him as garrulous, argumentative, funny, and profane. In his spare time he continued to work the fields with his father; the two were even awarded a medal from the Kremlin for threshing 889 tons of grain in 1948. In 1950, he moved to the capital to attend Moscow State University. His wardrobe consisted of one jacket, a few shirts, and two pairs of pants. The sights and sounds of the capital intoxicated Gorbachev—almost as much as did a striking philosophy student from western Siberia, Raisa Titorenko, whom he married in 1953.

After graduating from law school, Gorbachev returned to Stavropol, his native region, as an apparatchik responsible for promoting the Communist Party's programs and image. The human misery he encountered in the villages sowed doubts in him about the country's direction. Khrushchev's 1953 speech exposing the crimes of Stalin added to Gorbachev's disenchantment and fueled his desire for change. "I am simply overwhelmed with shame," he wrote to his wife. "Honestly I can't keep back my tears. . . . There's a great deal to be done. Our parents and thousands like them really deserve a better life."

Gorbachev's intelligence and energy earned the notice of the party leadership. He moved up the ranks of the local hierarchy, becoming the governor of the Stavropol region and a member of the Communist Party's powerful Central Committee. He traveled to Italy, Belgium, France, Czechoslovakia, and East Germany and began to read the writings of foreign leaders like François Mitterrand and Willy Brandt. His most important ally in the Kremlin was Andropov, then the head of the KGB, who arranged for Gorbachev to meet Brezhnev, the general secretary, at a train station in the Caucasus. Gorbachev impressed the aging Soviet leader, who made him agriculture secretary in 1978. At the time, the country's domestic food production was so dysfunctional that the country was draining its reserves of hard currency and maxing out oil production to pay for imported grain. When Gorbachev advocated a program of government incentives to encourage Russian farmers to increase their productivity, he was told the government was broke. To Gorbachev and other reformers, the solution was to scale back the country's colossal military spending and direct it toward meeting domestic needs. But such appeals fell on deaf ears, especially after Brezhnev's decision to invade Afghanistan. "The growth in military expenditure was far ahead of the growth in national income. Yet no attempt had ever been made to analyze that budget rationally," Gorbachev later wrote.

It was becoming clear to Gorbachev that to survive, the Soviet system needed dramatic, wholesale change—including a less hostile relationship with the West and a more open, responsive political culture. He surrounded himself with a group of like-minded reformers and cultivated allies among the Kremlin's younger generation. "Everything's rotten," Eduard Shevardnadze, a longtime ally and the head of the party in Georgia, told Gorbachev in 1984. "It has to be changed." Gorbachev got a brief chance to implement his ideas after Andropov succeeded Brezhnev as general secretary, but progress came to a halt when Andropov died. Gorbachev's allies pushed for him to take over, but the old guard of the Politburo chose Chernenko. "No matter who you talked to in those days, Gorbachev's name came up," wrote Anatoly Chernyaev, one of Gorbachev's aides. "We didn't want to believe it could be someone else."

As it turned out, they didn't have to wait long. Less than a year after he became general secretary, Chernenko was dead. When Gorbachev's election as the next leader of the Soviet Union was announced at the Kremlin on March 10, the hall erupted in applause. Three days later, Gorbachev met with U.S. Vice President George H. W. Bush and Secretary of State Shultz, who had come to Moscow for Chernenko's funeral. "The USSR has never intended to fight the United States and does not have such intentions now," he told the Americans. "There have never been such madmen within the Soviet leadership and there are none now." Shultz responded, "President Reagan told me to look you squarely in the eyes and tell you: 'Ronald Reagan believes this is a very special moment in the history of mankind.'" Later Shultz told the vice president, "We have an entirely different kind of leader in the Soviet Union than we have experienced before."

Shultz returned to Washington excited at the possibilities for a breakthrough with Gorbachev. On March 20, he and National Security Adviser Robert McFarlane met with Reagan in the Oval Office and urged the president to pursue a campaign of "quiet diplomacy—the need to lean on the Soviets but to do so one on one," as Reagan recorded in his diary. Five days later, Gorbachev sent Reagan a personal letter, expressing his belief that the two men shared the overriding goal "not to let things come to the outbreak of nuclear war." As Reagan had written to Brezhnev four years earlier, Gorbachev stressed the need "to create an atmosphere of trust between our countries" while insisting on the Kremlin's right to rule within its own borders as it saw fit. "All people have the right to go the way they have chosen themselves, without anybody imposing his will on them from outside." Responding to Reagan's invitation to visit Washington, extended by Shultz and Bush in Moscow, Gorbachev said he was eager for a personal meeting. He suggested that Reagan come to Moscow.

The two leaders were just beginning to get to know each other. On the day he took office, Gorbachev asked one aide for his opinion of the American president. Reagan "has a dream about being a 'great peacemaker president,'" the aide said. Reagan, who had long maintained the conviction that he could defuse the Cold War through personal dialogue, sought out assessments of Gorbachev.

After Margaret Thatcher met Gorbachev in December 1984 and declared, "This is a man I can do business with," Reagan invited her to Camp David to get her impressions. He made few public statements about U.S.-Soviet policy during the initial months of Gorbachev's tenure, instead letting his aides work out the arrangements for their first meeting. And yet if he was inclined to give the new Soviet leader a chance to pursue change, Reagan remained skeptical about how far Gorbachev was willing to go. The United States should not labor under illusions, he said. "Gorbachev will be as tough as any of their leaders," Reagan wrote after a meeting with Arthur Hartman, the new U.S. ambassador to Moscow. "If he wasn't a confirmed ideologue he never would have been chosen by the Politburo." Not long after, he received a breathless report from Armand Hammer, the oil magnate with long-running ties to Moscow. Hammer "feels I should go to Moscow for a meeting. He's convinced 'Gorby' is a different type than past Soviet leaders and that we can get along. I'm too cynical to believe that."

But Gorbachev *was* different. As he continued to issue private messages of conciliation, he embarked on a flurry of speeches and policy changes that signaled a new direction in Soviet conduct. In Moscow he hosted Tip O'Neill, the speaker of the house, and told him that "a fatal conflict of interest between our countries is not inevitable." He announced a reduction in the number of Soviet missiles in Europe. He ordered a moratorium on nuclear testing. To the military high command, Gorbachev declared his intention to withdraw Soviet forces from Afghanistan. In June, he replaced the aging foreign minister Andrei Gromyko with his friend Eduard Shevardnadze. Like Gorbachev, Shevardnadze believed that reforming the Soviet economy would be impossible without an easing of the rivalry between the superpowers. At their first meeting in Helsinki, Shevardnadze told Shultz he wanted to change "the image of the enemy." The rapport between the two diplomats was looser and less formal than anyone had witnessed before in a U.S.-

Soviet exchange. In June they agreed that the meeting between Reagan and Gorbachev would be held not in Washington nor Moscow. Instead the negotiators chose Geneva.

"I felt ready," Reagan later wrote of his meeting with Gorbachev. In the weeks leading up to the summit he had been prepped by Shultz about what to expect from the fifty-four-year-old Soviet leader. Gorbachev was smart and charming but unlikely to offer meaningful concessions, at least not right away. Though Reagan listened to Shultz, he harbored a confidence that he could handle Gorbachev once he got in a room with him. From the moment he arrived in Geneva, he was almost jittery with anticipation, finding it difficult to sleep.

On the morning of November 19, Reagan stepped outside the front door of the Fleur d'Eau villa, where the meetings were to take place. Displaying his instinct for showmanship, he chose not to wear an overcoat. When Gorbachev arrived in a hat, scarf, and a wool overcoat, he was startled to see the older man unprotected against the cold. The snapshot of the two men shaking hands played exactly as Reagan's image makers hoped: the whole world saw the American president looking more vigorous than a Soviet leader twenty years his junior. But in that first encounter, both Gorbachev and Reagan felt something else, an instant human connection that seemed to melt away their predecessors' icy wariness. "There was something likeable about Gorbachev," Reagan remembered. "There was warmth in his face and style." Gorbachev told an interviewer that immediately he found Reagan to be "a very authentic human being." "We shook hands like friends," he said.

The summit planners had scheduled fifteen minutes for Reagan and Gorbachev to meet alone and make opening statements, with only translators present. Instead they talked for an hour beside a roaring fire. Reagan remarked that they both came from modest backgrounds, and yet now they were here "with the fate of the world in their hands." He recited a Reaganism that often found its way into his speeches (including his address eighteen months later at the Brandenburg Gate): countries do not mistrust each other because of arms, they arm themselves because they mistrust each other.

Gorbachev replied that he was convinced relations between the two countries could improve. The Soviet people wished the United States no harm. Reagan said that if Russians got to know Americans they would find much in common. Americans hate war. "America is too nice a place when there is no war," he said. When Reagan gently chided Moscow for wanting to "shape developing countries to their own pattern," Gorbachev responded, "I don't wake up every day thinking about which country I'd like to now arrange a revolution in."

The warmth of that fireside chat faded when the two men joined their aides for plenary sessions. Reagan accused the Soviet Union of violating arms control agreements and rejecting past U.S. offers to reduce both sides' nuclear arsenals. Again he harped on Soviet intervention in the Third World, particularly Afghanistan. And he defended his cherished missile defense system, the Strategic Defense Initiative, which he knew Gorbachev was determined to kill. He insisted that SDI was not a weapon that posed a threat to the USSR, as Gorbachev characterized it; it was a purely defensive system against a potential common enemy. Disagreements over SDI would dominate most of the discussions for the next two days. At one point Reagan suggested to Gorbachev that they take a walk outside together and repair to a nearby boathouse to ease the tension.* They achieved no breakthroughs—"He's a caveman, a dinosaur!" Gorbachev told his advisers—but both men recognized they

---

* In an interview on the *Charlie Rose Show* in 2009, Gorbachev related an exchange with Reagan that had never been detailed before. Returning from the boathouse, Reagan asked Gorbachev, "What would you do if the United States were suddenly attacked by someone from outer space? Would you help us?" "No doubt about it," Gorbachev replied. To that, Reagan said, "We too." Gorbachev said, "It was an interesting moment."

had to keep talking. On the last day of the summit, during a parking lot exchange out of earshot of aides, they agreed to each visit the other's country. "To hell with the past," Reagan told Gorbachev on the night of November 20, before leaving Geneva. "We'll do it our way and get something done."

The president returned to Washington energized. Conservative columnists were already denouncing him for lying down for Gorbachev, but Reagan didn't care. He went before a joint session of Congress to pronounce the summit a success. "We didn't go in pursuit of some kind of phony détente," he said. But "every new day begins with possibilities . . . hope is a realistic attitude and despair an uninteresting little vice." He concluded with a vintage homage to the first Thanksgiving, when "Pilgrims and Indians huddled together on the edge of an unknown continent. Now here we are gathered together on the edge of an unknown future, but, like our forefathers, really not so much afraid." The lawmakers cheered the president, who was at the height of his popularity. "I haven't gotten such a reception," Reagan wrote that night, "since I was shot."

Both Reagan and Gorbachev believed they were charting a new course. They exchanged handwritten letters within days of returning home from Geneva. "I can assure you," Reagan wrote, in language that would have shocked hard-liners in his own administration, "that the United States does not believe that the Soviet Union is the cause of all the world's ills." In his response Gorbachev characterized the exchange of letters as "another one of our 'fireside talks.' I would truly like to preserve not only the spirit of our Geneva meetings, but also to go further in developing our dialogue." But sustaining the momentum proved difficult. The next twelve months were marked by hopes raised then dashed, initiatives proffered but not pursued—and, in Reagan's case, the Iran-contra affair, a political scandal that threatened to doom his presidency.

Both leaders also had to cope with national tragedies. On the morning of January 28, 1986, the president was in the Oval Office, working on a draft of his State of the Union speech. He was interrupted by Vice President Bush, Pat Buchanan, and Admiral John Poindexter, who had replaced McFarlane as national security adviser. "Sir, the Challenger just blew up!" Buchanan said. Seventy-three seconds into flight, the space shuttle Challenger had exploded on national television. In addition to six astronauts, the shuttle had been carrying Christa McAuliffe, a high school teacher who was to be the first civilian in space.

While Reagan and his aides watched coverage of the disaster, speechwriter Noonan started banging out lines for the speech the president would have to give to the nation. A White House aide provided her with notes of Reagan's reaction to the tragedy: "Pioneers have always given their lives on the frontier . . . but we must make it clear that life goes on." Noonan dug up a copy of a popular World War II poem called "High Flight" by John Gillespie Magee. She knew Reagan would recognize it. The last lines of his address from the Oval Office paid tribute to the fallen astronauts, quoting from Magee's poem. "We will never forget them, not the last time we saw them, this morning, as they prepared for their journey and 'slipped the surly bonds of earth' to 'touch the face of God.'" The next day Reagan confided to Noonan that he thought he blew the speech until the White House was deluged with phone calls and telegrams thanking him. "I guess it did work," he said.

Gorbachev's calamity was even more shattering. On April 26, two explosions at a nuclear power plant in Chernobyl caused a fallout equivalent to a 12-megaton nuclear blast, sending radioactive particles into Poland, Finland, and Sweden. Dozens of local residents had been sickened or died and tens of thousands were forced to evacuate. And yet the Kremlin did not acknowledge the disaster for more than forty-eight hours.

Gorbachev had initially listened to "experts" inside the Politburo who told him that the disaster was minor. When Hans Blix, the head of the International Atomic Energy Agency, arrived to tour the site, some Politburo members tried to block his visit, but Gorbachev overruled them. On May 14, Gorbachev finally went on television to declare, "A misfortune has befallen us." It was a breakthrough for political openness in Russia—thirteen major previous nuclear accidents had been concealed from the public—and for Gorbachev himself. Like nothing before, the disaster steeled his determination to eliminate the possibility of a nuclear conflict with the United States. "The accident Chernobyl showed again," he warned his countrymen, "what an abyss will open if nuclear war befalls mankind."

Chernobyl gave a boost to a concept that had long informed Gorbachev's thinking. The competition between the superpowers was at odds with true security, because the proliferation of nuclear weapons made the world inherently less safe. In the nuclear age, security could never be achieved through supremacy over foes, but only through cooperation with them. "Genuine equal security is guaranteed not by the highest possible, but by the lowest possible strategic balance," he said. He also recognized that social and economic progress in the Soviet Union required its integration in the global marketplace. He referred often to the growing interdependence of nations. "We live on one planet," he told comrades in the Politburo. "And we cannot preserve peace without America."

Gorbachev's confidence was growing. Audaciously, he proposed a total elimination of all nuclear weapons by the year 2000. Some of Reagan's advisers believed Gorbachev was trying to trick the president into abandoning SDI in return for arms reductions. They advised him not to respond to Gorbachev's overtures. The U.S. rebuffed Moscow's efforts to open broad negotiations and stepped up support for the anti-communist rebels in Latin America and Afghanistan. Reagan himself was torn. He liked Gorbachev personally, but he was not ready to trust his intentions.

When the Kremlin detained Nicholas Daniloff, a reporter for *U.S. News & World Report*, on trumped-up spying charges, the White House publicly denounced the Soviets, but privately agreed to release Gennadi Zakharov, a Soviet scientist who had been arrested by the FBI, in exchange for Daniloff. Shultz and Shevardnadze used their negotiations as a pretext to bring their bosses together again. "An idea has come to my mind to suggest to you, Mr. President," Gorbachev wrote in a letter to Reagan. He suggested that they not wait for their scheduled summit in Washington. Reagan agreed. They made plans to meet in Reykjavik, Iceland.

Rain lashed the windows of the Hofdi House, the hilltop mansion where the two leaders met on October 12, 1986. Gorbachev arrived determined to hammer out a sweeping arms control agreement. He immediately proposed a 50 percent reduction in strategic weapons across the board and the removal of all U.S. and Soviet missiles from Europe. Reagan, who tried to steer the conversation to human rights, was taken aback by Gorbachev's challenge. He told Gorbachev he agreed in principle with his ideas for deep arms cuts, then fell back on his favorite Russian phrase, *Doveryay, no proveryay*—trust, but verify. He said that the United States intended to continue testing a Star Wars defense system but would eventually share the technology with Moscow. Gorbachev countered by proposing that any research be limited "to the laboratory." After a day of negotiations, neither had compromised. Suddenly, on the afternoon of October 13, Reagan dropped his earlier insistence that arms cuts be limited to ballistic missiles—rather than all land-, sea-, and air-based weapons, as Gorbachev proposed. "It would be fine if we eliminated all nuclear weapons," Reagan said. The pronouncement stunned Shultz, who realized that Reagan was effectively proposing to end the arms race. He couldn't let the moment pass. "Let's do it," Shultz said.

Now it was Gorbachev's turn. Greatness was within reach, he told Reagan. He would sign a treaty "in two minutes" if Reagan agreed to limit SDI research to the laboratory. Reagan refused, saying he would be hammered by conservatives at home if he appeared to be compromising on Star Wars. "They're kicking my brains out," he said. Gorbachev "was asking him to give up the thing he'd promised not to give up." At one point he appealed to Gorbachev's sentimental side. He told him that he and Gorbachev "had the possibility of getting along as no two American and Soviet leaders ever had before." In ten years they could come back to Iceland to destroy the last two nuclear weapons on earth. "I'll be so old you won't recognize me. I'll say, 'Mikhail?' You'll say, 'Ron?'" "I may not be living after these ten," Gorbachev deadpanned.

As the clock neared 6:30 P.M., the warriors were still at an impasse. The discussion came down to whether a final agreement would restrict SDI testing to the "laboratory." "It's 'laboratory' or nothing," Gorbachev said, reaching for his briefcase. Reagan passed a note to Shultz, asking if he was wrong to turn Gorbachev down. Shultz shook his head. "The meeting is over," the president said. "Let's go, George." Outside, it was dark and Reagan's eyes were red with frustration. But before they parted, the two leaders embraced. "I don't know what else I could have done," Gorbachev said. Reagan climbed into his limousine. "You could have said yes," he said.

Shultz fought back tears as he briefed the press about how close the United States and the Soviet Union had come to an agreement. His shattered visage conveyed a sense of disaster, though he later wrote that "the achievements at the Reykjavik summit were greater than those in any U.S.-Soviet meeting before." Privately Shultz told Reagan, "You found a new world this weekend." After Reagan left, Gorbachev walked outside to gather his thoughts, then returned to speak to reporters at the Hofdi House. Gorbachev seemed sanguine, even elated. "Reykjavik is not a failure," he said. "It's a breakthrough." As he spoke, tears rolled down his wife's face.

On Air Force One returning to Washington, Dolan began composing a speech for Reagan to deliver on the outcome of the summit. As he rarely still did, Reagan rewrote substantial portions of the draft by hand. On October 13 he spoke to the nation from the Oval Office. "We are closer than ever before to agreements that could lead to a safer world without nuclear weapons," he said. By 11:30 the next morning the White House had received five thousand calls reacting to Reagan's speech; it reported a rate of "79 percent positive."

After Reykjavik, however, the political trajectories of the two leaders began to diverge. Gorbachev assured the Politburo that he was confident that the American president had no intention of attacking Moscow. He won support for deep cuts in defense spending and a timetable for ending the war in Afghanistan, which was claiming the lives of more than one thousand Soviet soldiers a year. Crucially, he told the countries of the Warsaw Pact, including East Germany, they could no longer depend on Moscow to safeguard their survival. They too would have to reform, or be cast aside by history.

Reagan, meanwhile, was embroiled in the most damaging episode of his presidency. In early November, reports surfaced of secret White House arms sales to Iran, in exchange for the release of U.S. hostages held in Lebanon. "Press are off . . . on a wild story built on an unfounded story originating in Beirut," Reagan wrote in his diary. But Reagan was forced to acknowledge a week later that the story was true: the U.S. had initiated weapons shipments to Iran, though Reagan denied that they were made in exchange for hostages.

There is considerable evidence, however, that Reagan explicitly intended for the arms sales to lead to the hostages' release. Even worse, administration officials, including Colonel Oliver North, deputy director for political-military affairs on the National Security Council, and National Security Adviser Poindexter, had authorized the diversion of profits from the arms sales to the contra rebels in Nicaragua, a clear violation of U.S. law. To cover up evidence of the Iran-contra connection, North and Poindexter ordered the shredding of some five thousand pages of documents relating to it. In late November, Attorney General Edwin Meese and chief of staff Donald Regan told the president about the illegal diversions to the contras. "This may call for resignations," Reagan wrote in his diary. The next day—in what historian Sean Wilentz calls "the worst performance of his Presidency"—Reagan appeared in the White House briefing room and read from a prepared statement, announcing the resignations of North and Poindexter. Then he left Meese at the mercy of the press. "They were like a circle of sharks," Reagan later fumed.

The president's fall in the eyes of the public was vertiginous. In early December, his approval ratings had dropped by 20 points. His pollster Dick Wirthlin informed him that "71% of the people like me and think I'm a nice fellow. But 60% don't think I'm telling the truth." The sudden erosion of his popularity left Reagan despondent. On Capitol Hill, there was talk of possible impeachment proceedings. Nancy urged him to fire Regan, who she believed had failed to protect the president from the scandal's fallout, but Reagan resisted. Instead he became more disengaged, occasionally failing to read briefing papers and spending more time in his private residence, watching old movies. As she prepared to leave the White House in late 1986, Noonan told an interviewer about her last meeting with Reagan in the Oval Office. "I had the sense for the first time of his aging," she said, "And the fact that he's an old man. An old man in a job that isn't an old man's job."

To even his most ardent supporters, Reagan's best days seemed behind him. In December, the White House announced that he would have to undergo surgery for prostate cancer in the new year. On December 10, a cable arrived at the State Department from Richard Burt, the U.S. ambassador to West Germany. It was marked EYES ONLY for Rozanne Ridgway, Shultz's top Western Europe hand. Burt presented an idea to his bosses at Foggy Bottom: Reagan should make a trip to Berlin. "As you know, our highest priority is a Presidential visit," Burt wrote, reminding Ridgway that during Chancellor Helmut Kohl's last visit to the White House, he had personally invited Reagan to come to West Germany. "For the President the most logical time to visit Berlin" would be the following June; he would be in Europe anyway, for the G-7 economic summit in Venice. It would coincide with the 750th anniversary of Berlin, which is "an important opportunity for us to strengthen our ties to the city." Having once worked at the State Department, Burt knew his cable was just one of the countless number that flowed in from diplomats in outposts all over the world. Perhaps his suggestion would never be read. But it was worth a try. With just two years left in the presidency, this was likely the last chance for Reagan to visit Berlin. And so Burt made one final pitch. "Berliners," he wrote, "consider it essential that he come."

Soviet soldiers raise the hammer-and-sickle over the Reichstag after the defeat of Nazi Germany and the fall of Berlin, May 2, 1945. Divided into four sectors by the conquering Allies, the city became a symbol of the division of Europe and the central proving ground of the U.S.-Soviet rivalry.

Harry S. Truman salutes U.S. troops in Berlin on July 21, 1945. At the Potsdam Conference with Winston Churchill and Josef Stalin, Truman disclosed the United States's intention to use the atomic bomb against Japan but avoided making major decisions over the future of Berlin.

A U.S. military plane delivers food and supplies to West Berliners in 1948 after Soviet forces blockaded the road and rail routes linking West Berlin to the rest of Germany. Lasting eleven months, the Berlin Airlift delivered 2.3 million tons of food to West Berlin and established an American commitment to the city that would endure for four decades.

On August 13, 1961, the communist leaders of East Germany, backed by Soviet Premier Nikita Khrushchev, sealed the border between East and West Berlin with three hundred tons of barbed wire. Two days later, an East German soldier named Conrad Schumann made this daring escape to West Berlin. The wire would eventually be replaced by concrete and become the Berlin Wall.

John F. Kennedy speaks before half a million people in front of the City Hall in West Berlin on June 26, 1963. The "Ich bin ein Berliner" speech whipped the masses into such a frenzy that the president later said that he feared that they might try to tear down the Berlin Wall. "We'll never have another day like this one," he told an aide.

6

Ronald Reagan eats lunch at his desk in the Oval Office six days after being sworn in as the country's fortieth president. Reagan came into office determined to end the Cold War. Though he authorized large increases in military spending and used tough rhetoric to condemn the behavior of the USSR, Reagan also pursued a personal dialogue with Soviet leaders and offered to negotiate with them.

Reagan addresses the British Parliament in London on June 8, 1982. In the speech he predicted that the West would leave the communist system on the "ash heap of history." The speech was drafted by Anthony Dolan, but Reagan, as he often did with major addresses, rewrote much of it by hand.

8

9

10

Despite differences in background, culture, and ideology, Ronald Reagan and Mikhail Gorbachev forged a relationship unlike any other between world leaders in the twentieth century. Their partnership halted the arms race and defused the U.S.-Soviet conflict. Scenes from three summits: a fireside talk in Geneva in 1985 (top); saying goodbye after failing to reach an arms reduction deal in Reykjavik, 1986; strolling through Moscow's Red Square in 1988.

11

Reagan meets with White House speechwriters on May 18, 1987, to discuss his trip to Europe, including the address he would give near the Berlin Wall. The draft of that speech set off a battle between the speechwriters and some of the president's advisers, who objected to numerous aspects of it, including the call for Gorbachev to tear down the Wall.

12

Reagan's visit to West Berlin in June 1987 was accompanied by disturbances in both sides of the city. In East Berlin, police clashed with hundreds of youths trying to hear a rock concert taking place on the other side of the Wall; it was the first public revolt against the communist regime in more than thirty years. Meanwhile, anti-American riots in West Berlin caused hundreds of thousands of dollars in damage and prompted the biggest police mobilization in the city's history.

Reagan delivers the "Remarks on East-West Relations at the Brandenburg Gate" on June 12, 1987. The speech lasted twenty-eight minutes. In his diary Reagan recorded that "I addressed tens & tens of thousands of people—stretching as far as I could see." Though it did not make major news in the United States when it was delivered, the speech would become the most famous of Reagan's presidency.

Germans celebrate at the Brandenburg Gate after the fall of the Berlin Wall, November 1989. Within a year the two Germanys became one. The democratic revolutions that spread across Eastern Europe in 1989 and subsequent breakup of the Soviet Union brought the Cold War to an end.

5. THE DINNER PARTY

R eagan would not be the only distinguished visitor in Berlin on its 750th birthday. Queen Elizabeth was on her way. Gorbachev planned a visit to East Berlin in May. The communist East German government announced "a year-long salute to [Berlin]'s history and culture," including the restoration of many historic buildings on the east side of the Wall. And yet the people of the city were in less mood to celebrate. By the start of 1987, resignation prevailed among Germans on both sides. Weariness with the Cold War and the forty-year division of Germany was widespread, but few had much hope that either would end. Public frustration simmered at the continued presence of foreign troops on German soil, including 250,000 Americans.

In West Germany, a peace movement secretly funded by the GDR seized on anxiety over the deployment of Pershing missiles to Western Europe to mobilize opposition to U.S. foreign policy. Anti-Reagan protests became a fixture of German street life. In one poll of West German public opinion, 49 percent said Gorbachev was concerned about "securing peace and disarmament," compared to 9 percent for Reagan. Meanwhile, West German officials explored ways to normalize relations with the GDR. The government approved a state visit by East German leader Erich Honecker—the first since the establishment of the GDR—and was rumored to be considering a proposal to allow East Berlin to officially become a part of the GDR in exchange for West Berlin's absorption into West Germany. Under such an arrangement, of course, the division of Berlin would become permanent.

No one wanted to talk about the Wall. At a forum in Bonn sponsored by the conservative Christian Democratic Union, U.S. ambassador Richard Burt shared the stage with his Russian counterpart, Yuli Kvitsinsky. Burt stressed the U.S.'s commitment to the eventual reunification of Germany. After the event, a pro-American member of the Bundestag approached him. "I really liked your talk," the politician said. "But that point about reunification, you really shouldn't make it." Burt asked why. "We all know that's not going to happen," the German said. "We know that the Wall isn't coming down."

Honecker seemed to benefit most from such fatalism. A lifelong communist, Honecker had overseen the building of the Berlin Wall before becoming the leader of the East German Communist Party in 1971. Gaunt, bespectacled, and enigmatic, Honecker embodied the weirdness of life in the GDR. His passions were few, outside of hunting, which he did inside the confines of the eight-hundred-acre settlement north of Berlin that housed members of the Politburo. Though he eased some strictures during the early years of his tenure—including lifting the regime's ban on blue jeans—Honecker rejected broader reforms. He told Gorbachev he had no interest in adopting Moscow's reform policies, known as perestroika and glasnost. As a result, the standard of living for East Germans remained stagnant well into the 1980s: they could drive only two models of cars; grocery store shelves offered little beyond canned meats and vegetables; fresh fruit was nonexistent. East Germany remained among the most politically repressive places in the communist bloc. The government built a vast network of prisons to detain intellectuals and political opponents. Under Honecker the Stasi grew to enlist more than one million informers, the vast majority of them ordinary citizens who spied on their friends and neighbors. Trying to escape Honecker's GDR could be fatal. East German border guards still observed a "shoot to kill" policy against any citizens trying to breach the Berlin Wall. When Lutz Schmidt, a twenty-four-year-old from East Berlin, tried to cross the Wall one foggy February night in 1987, the police shot him in the heart, killing him instantly. The Stasi cremated Schmidt's body and instructed his wife to tell her neighbors he died in a traffic accident.

And yet some East Germans were starting to push back. In cafés, churches, and living rooms in neighborhoods like East Berlin's Prenzlauer Berg, small bands of dissidents met secretly to discuss how to break the communists' grip. One of them was Gerd Poppe, an intellectual who had long been watched by the Stasi. He was barred from traveling outside the country and forced to work as a swimming pool attendant, even though he was trained as a physicist. In 1985 he founded the Initiative for Peace and Human Rights, a group dedicated to calling for the superpowers to disarm, but also to exposing the failures of the East German system. "We were different from peace movements of the West, which were fixated on the West as the enemy," he says. "That wasn't our theme. We were in favor of disarmament and relaxation—but not of the Communist regime being accepted as equal." For a while, Poppe's group struggled to gain attention. Poppe wrote pamphlets about conditions on the communist side of the Wall and slipped them to West German journalists and politicians. He couldn't communicate directly with ordinary East Germans, since the regime controlled all forms of media. His best bet was to stage small-scale demonstrations and hope to attract coverage on West German television, which was becoming available in the East.

Poppe and his fellow dissidents did tap a powerful urge among many residents of East Germany: the desire to get out. "People wanted the possibility of different lives. That's why freedom to travel was such a big thing. Everyone knew the Wall only existed to prevent GDR people from leaving." Restlessness was growing.

Would-be emigrants began to organize themselves. With a few dissident friends, Poppe purchased all the seats on a flight from Berlin to Prague, knowing that the authorities would not allow them to board. They invited Western journalists to follow them to the airport and film the police turning them away. The stunt landed Poppe and his friends in jail—"Everyone met up again at the Stasi prison," he says—but it publicized the fact that thousands of East Germans still lacked the basic freedom to travel.

Poppe let himself feel optimistic. "There was a sense of crisis coming," he recalls. "This was the start of when we tried to take it to the street." It would be years, however, before he discovered that the Stasi had plans of their own. The meticulous files kept by the Stasi on Poppe and his wife, Ulrike, detail the secret police's intention to destroy Poppe's career and break up his marriage. Ulrike "should be encouraged to believe that if she separates from her husband, she will be financially secure." A Stasi agent named "Harald" was assigned to develop "an intimate relationship" with Ulrike in order to "exacerbate the marriage crisis." (That operation failed.) Activists in the West may have viewed Ronald Reagan as the greatest threat to world peace. But to the totalitarian rulers of East Germany, the most dangerous enemy was the one within.

How much the Reagan administration sought to encourage, or even knew about, the signs of internal dissent in East Germany is debatable. Some officials did want Reagan to pressure Gorbachev to ease Moscow's hold on Eastern Europe. "The question of how to exploit one of the weaknesses of the Soviet empire—their unpopularity in Eastern Europe—had been a problem that American policymakers wrestled with and couldn't figure what to do about," says Stephen Sestanovich, who served on the National Security Council under Reagan and Bill Clinton. "It seemed to us as though Berlin offered an opportunity to push Gorbachev in an area where it would be hard to resist—and where you could capture some public enthusiasm in the Eastern Bloc." Teaming up with Nelson Ledsky, an Eastern Europe specialist at the State Department, Sestanovich drafted a document called "Berlin Without Barriers," which called for initiatives to promote greater ease of movement across the border "to show east Germans that there was more dynamism in the West and that they could get their government to change."

The idea met resistance from senior State Department officials and the U.S. embassy in Bonn, which didn't want to be seen to be telling the Germans what to do. The White House, meanwhile, was consumed with arms control talks and the growing Iran-contra scandal. As it had been for two decades, Berlin policy remained a relatively low priority. And so Sestanovich's proposal made little headway. In early 1987, Sestanovich left the government. Before he did, he handed his successor his files on "Berlin Without Barriers." "The thing we want is for Reagan to focus on the Wall," he said. "Our image is Reagan saying, 'Tear down this Wall.'"

It can be difficult to assess the credibility of such claims, made more than twenty years after the fact. No evidence exists to suggest that Sestanovich's "image" was widely discussed among other U.S. officials, if they knew about it at all. It's even more doubtful that the idea was floated to Reagan. But it's certain that he would have liked the sound of it. On the handful of occasions Reagan spoke publicly about the Berlin Wall before his visit to the city in 1987, he stressed his determination to see it torn down. In 1985, Reagan made the most controversial foreign trip of his presidency, a visit with Kohl to a German military cemetery near Bitburg, West Germany. Reagan made the trip at Kohl's urging, despite revelations that forty-nine members of the SS were buried there. Largely overlooked amid the furor over Bitburg was the speech he gave at a state dinner in his honor in Bonn. "Ahead of us may be a time when the artificial barriers that divide Germany, and indeed all Europe, are cast away, a time when there will be no need for weapons or barbed wire or walls in Berlin," he said. "These are not dreams. I believe from the bottom of my heart we have every reason for confidence."

A little more than a year later, Reagan returned to the subject in a series of statements marking the twenty-fifth year of the Wall's existence. In an interview with the German newspaper *Bild-Zeitung,* he said, "Dismantling the Wall would be a major step toward the improvement of east-west relations. . . . I would like to see the Wall come down today, and I call on those responsible to dismantle it." Five days later, at a news conference at the Hyatt Regency in Chicago, Reagan was asked if he would be "willing to go beyond rhetoric" and raise the matter of the Wall with Gorbachev. Reagan responded:

"I would have no hesitation whatsoever in a summit meeting to discuss this with the General Secretary. I think it's a wall that never should have been built. And I happen to believe that at the time that they started to put it up—and they started with wire, barbed wire, instead of a wall—that if the U.S. had taken the action it should have . . . that if we had gone in there and knocked down that wire then, I don't think there'd be a Wall today. . . . Isn't it strange that all of these situations where other people build walls to keep an enemy out, and there's only one part of the world and one philosophy where they have to build walls to keep their people in? Maybe they're going to realize that there's something wrong with that soon."

Parts of Reagan's off-the-cuff answer—the idea that the U.S. should have knocked down the Wall before it was built, and his assertion that "there's only one part of the world where they have to build walls to keep their people in"—were nearly identical to observations he had made about the Wall earlier in his career, in the 1967 debate with Robert Kennedy and in his 1982 trip to West Berlin. Viewed in that light, it is remarkable that some of his aides would later try to prevent Reagan from calling on Gorbachev to tear down the Wall—and that after he did, others claimed credit for coming up with the idea themselves. Only Reagan seemed aware that it was what he'd been saying all along.

The available documents do not help to pinpoint the precise date when the White House added Berlin to the itinerary for the president's trip to Europe in June. The memo from Ambassador Burt to Rozanne Ridgway, the assistant secretary of state for European affairs, suggests that as of December, a formal decision had not been made. The president's advisers knew that Reagan would find it hard to turn down a personal request from Kohl, who had sworn his "undying friendship" after Reagan's visit to the Bitburg cemetery in 1985. The embers of the Iran-contra scandal were beginning to cool, but Reagan's popularity remained lower than at any point in his presidency. To most of Washington he was a lame duck. Reagan's advisers knew he had few more opportunities to recapture the public imagination.

At 9:45 A.M. on February 4, Reagan met briefly in the Oval Office with Eberhard Diepgen, the mayor of West Berlin; the White House invited the occupant of the mayor's office to meet the president each year, to underscore the U.S.'s commitment to Berlin. Based on his diary entry that night, Reagan knew by the time he met Diepgen that he would be going to Berlin. The next day a brief item in the *New York Times*, sourced to an unnamed administration official, reported that Reagan planned to meet privately with Pope John Paul II in Rome on June 5, their first meeting since 1982. The same item reported that on June 12, the president would make a stop and give an address in Berlin. First, though, the White House had to determine where in the city Reagan would give his speech, and who would write it.

The Reagan White House was obsessed with the details of stagecraft. For much of the presidency, the job of orchestrating the "visuals" for Reagan's appearances belonged to Michael Deaver, the president's longtime adviser. Deaver had overseen the White House's Office of Presidential Advance, a group of Reagan loyalists who cut their teeth working on Reagan's gubernatorial campaigns and pored over the backdrops for his public events like Hollywood directors scouting set locations. "We spent a lot of our time on how things would look on the front page of the *New York Times*, or on TV," says Andrew Littlefair, who worked in the Advance Office for four years. "Because if it doesn't look right, then what the president's saying doesn't get heard or seen. He might as well not have been there." The director of the Advance Office was Bill Henkel, who had held the same job under Nixon and Ford. After Deaver's departure from the White House in 1985, Henkel took over the planning of Reagan's trips. In January, Henkel flew to Europe to survey possible sites for Reagan's appearances during his upcoming trip to Italy, for the G-7 Economic Summit, and to Germany, for Berlin's 750th birthday celebration.

On February 6, Henkel sent a confidential memo to chief of staff Regan and Frank Carlucci, who had replaced Poindexter as national security adviser, presenting a "Trip Concept" for Reagan's European swing. "The trip contains events that may match some of the great moments of previous foreign trips . . . the memories and images of which are ingrained in the consciousness of many Americans still today," Henkel wrote. "The trip will provide platforms for the President to call for the lowering of physical, economic and emotional barriers." The speech in Berlin was central to delivering that message, Henkel wrote. "Berlin itself as a metaphor. It is a symbol of the commitment of the West to freedom."

Henkel drafted a "proposed outline" for the trip—a document that is remarkable to read today, since the eventual itinerary in June would track, almost to the minute, with what Henkel laid out five months earlier. Upon arriving in Berlin from Venice, Henkel suggested, the president and first lady should "participate in events with great historical and emotional background and impact." First he would go to the Reichstag, where he would be greeted on the steps by Chancellor Kohl. Inside the former Parliament building, he would meet a group of German women known as the "Rubble Ladies," for their role in rebuilding Berlin after World War II. From there "the President could move to a balcony overlooking the Berlin Wall, east Berlin and the 'Crosses on the Wall,'" which honored those killed trying to escape from the East. Henkel estimated that Reagan would leave the Reichstag at 1:45 in the afternoon and proceed to "a speech site near the Brandenburg Gate—which, incidentally, is separated by the Wall from West Berlin." Positioning Reagan against such a backdrop was critical to the success of the speech. "The symbolism of the Gate as a means of passage . . . will accord the President an historic opportunity to use the lessons (and mistakes) of the past as a guide for the future," Henkel wrote.

As Henkel sketched out his vision for a "Brandenburg Address," the duty of convincing the Germans to allow Reagan to deliver it there fell to John Kornblum. A ruddy, rumpled career diplomat, Kornblum was a fluent German speaker who had run the State Department's Central Europe desk before being posted to Berlin in 1985. As soon as the White House confirmed the president's visit, Kornblum began lobbying city officials to allow Reagan to speak near either the Reichstag or the Brandenburg Gate, Berlin's most recognizable landmarks. The reaction to Brandenburg, Kornblum later wrote, was "swift and negative: security could not be guaranteed, the venue would provoke the East . . . they did not want the speech to be given anywhere near the Berlin Wall." The Germans "were just petrified that standing there in front of the Brandenburg Gate would send an aggressive signal to Gorbachev," Kornblum says. But Kornblum was determined that Reagan give his speech at the Gate. When he continued to push the idea, officials in the West German Foreign Ministry tried appealing over his head. "They sent direct messages to the White House saying 'This is terrible, and you shouldn't do this.' But the Reagan people loved the thing."

Since Berlin remained under four-power control, the U.S. could make the rules.

In early March, members of the White House advance team arrived in West Berlin on a second scouting mission. One member of the team, James Hooley, asked first to see the square in front of the City Hall, where John F. Kennedy gave his "ich bin ein Berliner" speech. "We weren't going to compete in that location," Hooley says, "but Kennedy had all those people there. So we needed a big crowd." Kornblum, acting as the tour guide for Hooley's team, took them to see the Reichstag, which West German officials were eager for Reagan to visit, even if it held little visual appeal to the Americans. "It was essentially a waste of time, but we had to do it," Kornblum says. From there the delegation walked down a ramp leading to a plaza a few hundred yards west of the Brandenburg Gate. The base of the Gate was obscured by the Berlin Wall. "I can remember the group of us standing there saying, you know, 'Why not right here?'" Hooley says. Some of the U.S. consular officials accompanying Hooley's team seemed to disapprove, but not Kornblum. To seal the deal, Kornblum drove further down the boulevard, to give the advance team a full view of the Wall, scarred with graffiti and barbed wire, with the six columns of the Brandenburg Gate rising behind it. "Just look at this," he said. "This is going to be the most dramatic scene that President Reagan has ever had."

Kornblum says, "I sold it to them with the camera angles." And it worked. For anyone who has seen a photograph or watched footage of the "Tear Down This Wall" speech, it is impossible to separate the visual picture of the Brandenburg Gate looming behind Reagan from the words he delivered; the image has become as indelible as the message. "I'm sure there are other cases," Hooley says. "But it's the only time I know of where a speech that became so significant was driven not necessarily from a policy decision but by the site selection. . . . If we'd been two miles away, there would have been no line. I don't think they could have written, 'Tear down *that*

Wall.'" Andrew Littlefair adds, "If we ended up asking Mr. Gorbachev to tear down the Wall and we were in the Intercontinental ballroom in Berlin, well, what does that do for you?"

Hooley took snapshots of the site to show Reagan's aides in Washington. Where the president would speak when he went to Berlin was no longer in doubt. The battle over what he would say was just beginning.

Dolan wanted to write the Berlin speech. He was now running the speechwriting office, having assumed the job after chief of staff Regan fired Ben Elliott. "But if you're the head speechwriter you can't grab everything," Dolan says. "It's unhealthy." Noonan would have been a likely candidate to write it, but by then she had left the White House. Dolan finally decided to give the speech to Peter Robinson, a thirty-year-old who had joined the speechwriting staff in 1985 but had yet to write a major address. This would be his chance, Dolan felt, "to do a breakout speech."

Robinson had grown up in Vestal, New York, in a middle-class Catholic household. His father, a World War II veteran who saw combat in the Pacific, supported the family doing a string of odd jobs. Peter attended Dartmouth, paying his tuition with student loans. In college he found himself surrounded by well-heeled classmates from prep-school backgrounds. Robinson worked hard to compensate, keeping long study hours more typical of premed students. "If I did badly at Dartmouth, I'd have felt as though I'd let down the whole town of Vestal," he later wrote. After graduating, he spent two years at Oxford and tried writing a novel but gave up halfway through. In the spring of 1982 Robinson wrote a letter to William F. Buckley, Jr., whom he had met at Dartmouth, asking if he knew of possible job opportunities. Buckley put Robinson in touch with his son, Christopher, who was leaving his job as a speechwriter for Vice President Bush. Buckley suggested that

Robinson replace him. After two weeks of interviews he was hired. "I got a job as a White House speechwriter," Robinson recalled, "without ever having written a speech in my life."

Robinson remembers that upon arriving in the capital, he felt "like a medieval peasant or monk who suddenly found himself in Rome." Outside the office, he led a bachelor's existence, renting an apartment on Massachusetts Avenue and spending most evenings rowing, playing squash, or going out for beers. After working for Bush for eighteen months, Robinson was hired to join the president's speechwriting staff. By the spring of 1987, Robinson was the third-longest-serving writer in the White House. He remained self-deprecating and eager to please. He made a point to attend in person any speech he had written for the president. He steeped himself in Reagan's favorite jokes and anecdotes. "To be in that White House and do your job as a speechwriter you're really studying one human being—the way his mind worked, everything from his mannerisms to his policy decisions, from the low to the high," he says. "By the time I wrote the [Berlin] speech I'd had five years of watching that guy very closely."

In early April, Dolan told Robinson he would be writing the Brandenburg Gate speech, though he gave Peter few instructions about what it should say. "The guidance was very, very thin," Robinson says. "It was our job not just to do first-draft writing, but first-draft thinking about what it would be appropriate for the president to say." Peter met with Hooley, who showed him photographs of the spot the advance team had chosen for the speech. He retrieved a tape of Kennedy's Berlin speech, which would serve as a "negative model" for his draft; he didn't want Reagan's speech to be compared to Kennedy's. "He's not going to get one million people in the streets," Robinson told himself. Then he decided to go to Berlin.

The advance team was due to travel to Europe in mid-April, to finalize Reagan's itinerary. Robinson went along. The group flew in the plane that had brought the body of the slain Kennedy back from Dallas in 1963. The first stop was Rome, where Robinson had almost nothing to do. He went out with friends, visited museums and took a motorcycle tour of the city. "Your tax dollars at work," he later joked. After five days in Rome and a brief stop in Venice, the site of the economic summit, Robinson and the advance team arrived in West Berlin. After the idyll of Italy, the cold grimness of Berlin was startling. The Wall was not visible from Robinson's hotel on the Kurfürstendamm, the main shopping drag in West Berlin—"But boy, you could just feel somehow that you were surrounded by a hostile presence." After arriving, Robinson received a fifteen-minute briefing from Kornblum. In his memoir, published in 2003, Robinson wrote that Kornblum told him that "the President would . . . have to watch himself. No chest thumping. No Soviet-bashing. And no inflammatory statements about the Wall. West Berliners . . . had long ago gotten used to the structure that encircled them." Kornblum says he doesn't recall the details of his meeting with Robinson, but disputes the suggestion that he gave Robinson any specific instructions about what to put in Reagan's speech.

What Kornblum did not tell Robinson was that he had written a speech draft of his own, which he sent to his bosses at the State Department on March 6. Kornblum's draft—which has recently been declassified—runs through developments in East-West relations since Reagan's previous visit to Berlin and outlines several modest steps to encourage "openness" in the city, such as loosening travel restrictions, promoting cultural exchanges, and allowing more commercial flights into Berlin. The draft calls for an end to the division of Germany. And it includes two references to the Wall. "Your courage and your unity will ensure that—one day—this ugly Wall will disappear," reads one section, to be addressed to Berliners. A passage near the end says, "Europe must be reunited. Barriers to contact must be torn down. We should begin with the ugly Wall which divides this great city."

Kornblum's draft was circulated inside the State Department and among staffers at the National Security Council. It was accompanied by a cover letter that highlighted the draft's aim "to present a major statement of President Reagan's . . . vision for a dynamic Europe which is not doomed to division." The letter goes on to say that "Germans especially fear moving too far too fast. They shy away from the hint of confrontation." An internal NSC document records that Kornblum's draft was forwarded to the White House speechwriters on April 28. But there's no sign that they read it. Only after Robinson had composed his own draft of the speech did he learn that Kornblum's existed. Some of Kornblum's policy proposals would find their way into the final address, but not much of his language did. Even so, the draft's specific references to the Wall appear to support Kornblum's recollection of his meeting with Robinson. It seems unlikely that Kornblum would tell Robinson that there should be "no inflammatory statements about the Wall," when he had already written some himself.

The rest of Robinson's thirty-six-hour trip to Berlin left a deeper impression on him. After meeting Kornblum, Robinson took a tour of the city aboard a U.S. Air Force helicopter. From above Robinson was struck by the contrasts between East and West: "on one side lay movement, color, modern architecture, crowded sidewalks, traffic. On the other lay a kind of void." The east side of the Wall revealed itself to be a maze of guard posts, barbed wire, and dog runs. Later he toured the Reichstag and, further up the Strasse des 17 Juni, walked past the monument to Soviet troops killed in World War II. "There were a couple Red Army soldiers goose-stepping back and forth," Robinson says. "It was creepy and surreal. It had just a sense of power, kind of the brutal power of history. And that shook me." The drama of the city's past and the tension of its present were intimidating. For the first time, Robinson began to worry about what, exactly, the speech would say.

That night, Robinson slipped away from the rest of the U.S.

delegation to attend a dinner party in Dahlem, a leafy district thirty minutes southwest of the city center. The hosts were a German couple named Dieter and Ingeborg Elz. The Elzes had lived in Washington for twenty years, when Dieter worked at the World Bank. When they moved back to Berlin in the mid-1980s, they were shocked at how many people in the city had accepted the Wall as an immutable fact of life. And unlike most of their neighbors, they admired Ronald Reagan. The Elzes assembled a group of friends to meet Robinson. They broke the ice by talking about things like the weather, German wine, and the cost of housing. When the discussion turned to politics, Robinson began scribbling in his black hardbound notebook. Anti-Americanism among young Germans was fading, one guest said, but Reagan's visit would likely spur some protests.

Then the division of Berlin was discussed. "The difference between JFK and now: no immediate danger," Robinson recorded in his notes. "Talk instead about the long-term march of liberty—and the patience it requires." A guest named Eberhard von Puttkamer, an official in the West German government, drew a sketch in Robinson's notebook to illustrate the symbolic significance of the Brandenburg Gate: the Gate and the buildings east of it constituted the historic heart of the city, and yet the area remained inaccessible to West Berliners. It was as if the communists had captured downtown Washington, including Pennsylvania Avenue, the Capitol, the White House, and the monuments on the Mall—and the West had Chevy Chase and Bethesda. Robinson says that "I began to understand the meaning of what that meant. For West Germans, the Brandenburg Gate was the beginning of what they could no longer have."

Robinson's notes show that the guests agreed that Reagan should "address Berliners as a whole, East and West alike. But: not just the sadness of the East, but a splendid city in its own right." When Robinson asked them if they had become resigned to living with the Wall, the talk grew more emotional. "My sister lives twenty miles in that direction," one man said. "I haven't seen her in more than two decades. Do you think I can get used to that?" Another man added that "Seven hundred fifty years are a long time in German history. Forty-five years of separation is almost nothing. The division is one we do not recognize." A third guest related an anecdote about walking past the same East German border guard each morning—someone with whom he shared a history, culture, and language—and feeling like "one of us is a zookeeper and the other is an animal, and I am never certain which is which." After a few more minutes, the hostess, Ingeborg Elz, spoke up. "If this man Gorbachev is serious with his talk of perestroika and glasnost, he can prove it," she said. "He can get rid of this Wall."

Robinson seized on the phrase immediately. That's big, he thought to himself. That's good. He paraphrased Elz's comments in his notes: "If the Russians are willing to open up, then the Wall must go. Open the Brandenburg Gate." The dinner lasted another hour and Robinson probed for more color for the speech. The guests suggested he borrow from West German president Richard von Weizsäcker, who had said that "the German question remains open as long as the Brandenburg Gate is closed." Robinson picked up a few phrases popular among Germans, like the title of a Marlene Dietrich song, "Ich hab noch einen Koffer in Berlin" (I always leave a suitcase in Berlin).

Peter left Berlin the next day. He later composed a thank-you note to the Elzes that ended with the Dietrich line. The dinner party had been the highlight of his two-week trip, he wrote. "What came across most powerfully was the depth of feeling—the love— that the Berliners in your home had for their city," he told the Elzes. Even more important, he returned to Washington with what he believed could be a guiding theme for Reagan's speech. "There was always a certain amount of diplomatic stuff that would go in any foreign policy speech," he says. "But what the speechwriters were always trying to do was make it fresh, make it true to Ronald Reagan." One way or another, Robinson decided on his way home, Reagan's speech at the Brandenburg Gate should include a clear, direct call to bring down the Berlin Wall.

It was a simple idea. Making it real would prove more difficult than Robinson ever imagined.

6. "A MISSED OPPORTUNITY"

Tony Dolan worked on the second floor of the Old Executive Office Building, the hulking nineteenth-century edifice that Harry Truman once called "the greatest monstrosity in America." Dolan didn't mind. From the window of his corner office, he had a view of the magnolia trees along Lafayette Square, the West Wing of the White House, and, beyond it, the obelisk of the Washington Monument. Dolan's office had twelve-foot ceilings, a couch, and a marble fireplace. It was huge. "Bigger than some small hotel lobbies," Dolan recalls.

Robinson walked into Dolan's office as soon as he returned from Berlin. Dolan had his cowboy boots propped up on the desk.

"Tony, here's what I'd like the president to say," Robinson began. "Tear down the Wall."

Dolan looked up at Robinson. He pushed his chair back from the desk, until he was drenched in the sunlight streaming through the windows. "My God, Peter," Dolan remembers saying. "What a great idea. What a wonderful idea."

It was not unique. Staffers at the National Security Council had been working for more than a year with officials at the State Department to draft a Presidential Initiative on Berlin. Two weeks before Robinson's trip to Berlin, the interagency group met to discuss how to get those ideas into Reagan's speech in June. On April 8, Fritz Ermarth, the NSC's senior director for Soviet and European affairs, sent a memo to the new deputy national security adviser, a U.S. Army lieutenant general named Colin Powell. Ermarth's memo reported on the working group's proposals for "political, social and cultural initiatives on Berlin, some or all of which would be appropriate to include in the President's June 12 address in Berlin." Perhaps Reagan could promote Berlin as a host for important international conferences, or even the Olympic Games. He could announce some measures to boost commerce in West Berlin. "Finally, in the spirit of 'glasnost,' " Ermarth wrote, "the President might call on the East to tear down the Wall."

Tracing the birth of successful policies in a bureaucracy is tricky. Sometimes they spring from a single fountainhead, a lone official's sudden inspiration about how to do things differently. More often, though, they are group efforts, generated by a number of people thinking along the same lines—sometimes without even knowing what the others are up to. The same goes for speeches. The most memorable phrases in presidential history have rarely flowed from a solitary pen (with the legendary exception of Lincoln's Gettysburg Address), but instead were shaped by and borrowed from multiple sources. Variations on FDR's "fear itself" line had been articulated by Americans ranging from Henry David Thoreau in 1884 ("Nothing is so much to be feared as fear") to the chairman of the U.S. Chamber of Commerce in 1931 ("In a condition of this kind, the thing to be feared most is fear itself"). Roosevelt's own speechwriter, Raymond Moley, later said he lifted the phrase from a department store ad. For JFK's first inaugural, Ted Sorensen solicited advice from luminaries like Adlai Stevenson, Walter Lippmann, and John Kenneth Galbraith; it was Galbraith who crafted the oft-quoted line, "Let us never negotiate out of fear. But let us never fear to negotiate." Sorensen and Kennedy developed the "Ask not" anastrophe from similar statements made by JFK during the campaign, which in turn borrowed from Kennedy's study of the history of political rhetoric. In his authoritative book on presidents and their speechwriters, *White House Ghosts*, Robert Schlesinger wrote that "seeking the origin of a specific phrase is akin to straining to find the source of the first noise in an echo chamber. It is unknowable—and while the search makes for interesting historical trivia, the answer is ultimately irrelevant."

The same could be said for "Tear Down This Wall." Robinson's dinner with the Elzes in West Berlin was the first time the idea of removing the Wall had burst into *his* mind—like "a detonation" he would say later. Even then, he would take weeks to find the right words to express it. And yet it's now evident that a range of people inside the U.S. government had also come to the conclusion that Reagan needed to call for the Berlin Wall to come down. *How* to do it would be the source of considerable argument over the following weeks. But a number of U.S. officials—not only Robinson, Dolan, and the speechwriters, but also people like Steve Sestanovich, John Kornblum, Nelson Ledsky, Fritz Ermarth, and others—thought Reagan should. They might not have known when the Berlin Wall would collapse, but they believed it was possible. The world was changing. Maybe it was time.

The winter of 1987 had been the unhappiest time of Ronald Reagan's presidency. His failure to provide a full accounting of his involvement in the Iran-contra scheme had battered his standing with the American people. His diary entries during that time are a catalogue of gloom, which was compounded by a slow recovery from prostate surgery. He displays only cursory interest in subjects other than his sagging poll numbers. "Dick Wirthlin came by with poll numbers," he writes on January 15. "Just a slight drop—like 55 instead of 57% on job rating . . . nothing to get excited about."

Six weeks later he records that "79% like me but my job rating has fallen to 44% in light of the Iran affair." The scandal and Reagan's diminished stature were damaging the U.S.'s standing abroad too; a *Newsweek* poll found that support for the United States among Europeans had reached an all-time low. In both Britain and Germany, less than one-third of those polled believed the U.S. was serious about stopping the arms race.

Some of Reagan's backers tried to rally him. "You must re-focus the nation's attention on the central issue of Freedom vs. Communism," Tom Ellis, a conservative supporter, wrote in a letter to Reagan. "You can be—you must be—the Churchill of your time." At Nancy's urging, Reagan gave a speech to the nation from the Oval Office admitting he had traded arms for hostages. The White House switchboard received more phone calls in support of Reagan than for any other speech. "Even the TV bone pickers . . . said nice things about it," Reagan wrote. In overnight polls his job approval rating jumped ten points. The bounce seemed to energize the president, as did the staff housecleaning at the White House. Reagan brought in a new national security adviser, Frank Carlucci, and chief of staff, former Senate majority leader Howard Baker. With Democrats controlling Congress and looking ahead to the 1988 presidential election, Reagan's team knew that if anything was to be achieved in the remaining eighteen months of his presidency, it would be in foreign policy. In the words of one biographer, Lou Cannon, "He sought solace by playing the role of statesman."

Arms control talks between the United States and the Soviet Union had stalled after Reykjavik, when Reagan and Gorbachev nearly agreed to eliminate all nuclear weapons. But in early 1987 Gorbachev announced that he would accept a treaty to get rid of all intermediate-range nuclear missiles (known as INF—Intermediate-Range Nuclear Forces) in Europe. He no longer insisted on the limits on missile defense that had doomed the talks in Reykjavik. Reagan sensed an opportunity. He instructed Shultz to go to Moscow and deliver a letter to Gorbachev. "I can recall at Geneva sitting before a fireplace and commenting that you and I were in a unique position," Reagan wrote in longhand. "Together we can make a difference in the future course of world events. Let us pray that you and I can continue our dialogue so that the future will be one of peace and prosperity for both our nations and for the world."

Shultz's trip to Moscow was an eye-opener. In meetings with government officials, journalists, and dissidents, he sensed a mood of hope and openness that was unprecedented in postwar Russia. He visited a group of intellectuals at a dacha outside Moscow. A writer told him he was publishing a banned novel that he had written twenty years earlier. A producer was staging plays that could never before have been put on. "I said, 'Well aren't you a little afraid that something that has been turned on can be turned off?'" Shultz recalls. "And they said, 'No, there's too much momentum. It's going to be very hard to turn off.'" Later Shultz gave an interview to a Russian television talk show. He harshly criticized the Soviet invasion of Afghanistan and called for Gorbachev to pull out. The Kremlin allowed the entire interview to be aired. "I said to myself, that would never have happened otherwise. Something is changing."

Shultz flew to Reagan's ranch in California to brief him on the trip. Gorbachev had repeated his willingness to eliminate missiles in Europe and suggested he would come to Washington to sign an arms reduction treaty. Reagan was thrilled. He told Shultz that he had long dreamed of giving a Soviet leader a helicopter tour of America, in which he would show his counterpart the material bounties enjoyed by ordinary Americans and that the Russian people were missing. "I look forward to and hope we can have a summit . . . and that Mr. Gorbachev and I can complete an historic agreement," Reagan told reporters gathered at the ranch. That night he wrote in his diary, "There is reason to believe we may be on the path to some arms reduction."

But not everyone was on board. Reagan's eagerness to do business with Moscow enraged some of his former allies on the right, who mistrusted Gorbachev and believed Reagan was selling out his principles. "For the first time, I and my colleagues need to take very serious issue with you," Reagan's friend William F. Buckley wrote to the president, two weeks after Shultz returned from Moscow. Buckley enclosed the latest issue of his magazine, *National Review*, which included a piece by Richard Nixon and Henry Kissinger criticizing Reagan's moves toward a deal with Gorbachev. "You will discover in it the depths of our anxiety," Buckley wrote. The criticism stung Reagan. On May 5, he replied to Buckley's letter by pointing out that the Soviets were agreeing to ideas, such as the "zero-zero" elimination of short-range missiles, which Reagan himself had proposed six years earlier. For all Gorbachev's charm, Reagan insisted his position on the Soviets remained the same. He told Buckley, "I have not changed my belief we are dealing with an 'evil Empire.'"

Later in the afternoon Reagan met with his political advisers to plot out the remaining months of his presidency "and all the important things we seek to achieve." Nancy returned to Washington after two days in New York. After six long years in the White House, she was the only person with whom Reagan truly felt close. "Mommies home," Reagan wrote in his diary before going to bed. "Thank heaven."

As the president fended off attacks from the right, Peter Robinson was having struggles of his own. He labored over the organization of the speech and how to phrase the language about the Wall. He made at least five false starts, writing a few pages and then starting over again. "Can't seem to find the organization in one's mind," he wrote in his journal on May 6. He jogged and then rowed on the Potomac to clear his head. The next day was better. "Made headway," he wrote. He outlined broad themes for the speech—"Make necessary connection between freedom and success"; "Show future of world"; "End on religious note"—but the Wall was the dominant motif. "Will this Wall stand or fall?" he writes in the opening of one version. Later he invokes Kennedy's 1963 speech, even though he had told himself to stay away from it: "In this, our fervent desire to see this Wall come down, we are all of us Berliners." A long section on the history of postwar Europe follows, highlighting contrasts between the socialism of the East with the market democracy in the West. In this draft, it takes a full thirteen pages for the payoff line to appear: "If you truly believe in glasnost, Herr Gorbachev, bring down this Wall."

As he wrote and rewrote, Robinson struck upon another theme he liked. West Berliners lived in an encircled city, yet they chose to stay there. Why? "In a word, what keeps you here is love . . . a love that says yes to this city's beauty, to the opportunities it offers, to its future, to freedom." But when it came to the Wall, Robinson couldn't quite get the wording right. Yet another draft reads, "Let me promise: If Mr. Gorbachev is willing to take down this Wall, I will meet him here, here at the Brandenburg Gate. We can begin this work together." This time Robinson wrote, "Herr Gorbachev, take down this Wall." The line was still buried deep in the speech.

After working for a week, Peter gave a draft to Dolan. A few minutes later Dolan was in Peter's office. "It's just not good enough," Dolan said, throwing the pages down on the desk. The usually genial Robinson shot back. "Why do you say it's not good enough?" he asked. "What specifically?" "The whole thing," Dolan replied. He told Robinson to take the weekend off and "come back at it with fresh eyes." Robinson tried again. For two nights he barely slept. "Worked on Berlin," he wrote in his journal on May 11. "Kept binding up, [largely] because one cared so vy. much about it."

Robinson had a tight deadline. After Robinson's return from Berlin, Dolan had summoned the speechwriters to his office to discuss their assignments for the upcoming European trip. Dana Rohrabacher, the longest-tenured writer after Dolan, recalls feeling that "something big was about to happen." Robinson gave an account of his trip to Berlin: the meeting with Kornblum, the visit to the Brandenburg Gate, the dinner with the Elzes. After listening to Robinson, "we all agreed, this is the time that the president has to demand that the Berlin Wall come down," Rohrabacher says. "If we're going to have better relations, the Berlin Wall has to come down." Dolan told his team that the Berlin speech had the potential to be "THE statement of the Cold War." But he anticipated a fierce battle with foreign policy hands who would try to water down the president's language. Dolan told the speechwriters he wanted to give Reagan speech drafts for the European trip before the president left for the weekend on May 15; if the speeches were delivered at once, it would be harder for Reagan's senior staff to go through all of them. Dolan believed that if Reagan saw the passage about tearing down the Wall, he would endorse it, and at that point it would be nearly impossible to take the line out. "We got every speech done for the European trip a week before they were due. We were doing more than double or triple our regular load of work," Rohrabacher says. "And of course all of that work was done to protect one page of one speech, which was, 'Mr. Gorbachev, tear down this Wall.'"

Working himself to exhaustion, Robinson managed to complete a revised draft in time for Dolan's May 15 deadline. At 1:45 on the afternoon of May 18, the five speechwriters—Dolan, Rohrabacher, Robinson, Clark Judge, and Josh Gilder—met with the president in the Oval Office. With them was Tom Griscom, a thirty-eight-year-old former newspaper reporter from Tennessee, who had succeeded Pat Buchanan as White House communications director. A photograph of the meeting captures Reagan sitting cross-legged in an armchair, with Griscom and the speechwriters filling two sofas: pens poised, legal pads in hand. Robinson is leaning forward, listening intently, trying to soak up every moment of this rare audience with the president.

Griscom asked Reagan if he had any thoughts on the speeches for his European trip. In Rome, he would make brief remarks before meeting with Pope John Paul II, a vital ally in the struggle to liberate Eastern Europe. That speech had been assigned to Gilder, who asked the president what role religion could play in changing the communist system. "He went into this really beautiful discourse on how change in the Soviet Union would have to be a spiritual awakening," Gilder says. "He talked about it beautifully. I took notes as fast as I could." It was a speechwriter's dream: the president practically dictated the whole thing for Gilder. "It wasn't a long speech—just about four pages. And so I tacked on an intro and an ending. The middle two pages were just straight Reagan." Robinson wasn't as lucky. His speech was the last one discussed. When Griscom asked Reagan what he thought of the Berlin draft, Reagan responded that he liked it. Robinson wanted more. "I've been over there," he told the president. "What do you want to say to people on the other side of the Wall?" Reagan thought for a moment. "Well, there's that passage about tearing down the Wall," he said. "That's what I'd like to say to them." The meeting had lasted twenty-one minutes. Robinson was disappointed that Reagan didn't offer anything new, but as they left the Oval Office, Dolan knew he had gotten what he came for: the president's endorsement would be his most powerful weapon in the bureaucratic battles to come.

Two days after the session with the president, Robinson delivered a revised draft to Dolan. He had inserted a fresh anecdote at the end, about how the East German government had removed a cross from the sculpture that sits on top of the Brandenburg Gate and replaced it "with a communist wreath." Later, when the communists built the city's highest structure, the television tower above Alexanderplatz, they were stunned to discover what they perceived as an architectural flaw. "Even today when the sun strikes that dome—the dome that towers over all Berlin—the light makes the sign of the cross." There were other significant changes. Robinson had condensed much of the historical section and moved up the challenge to Gorbachev. "If you seek liberalization—if you seek glasnost—come to Berlin. Come here, to this Wall. *Herr Gorbachev, machen Sie dieses Tor auf.*" The translation of the phrase was in brackets, but Peter did not intend for Reagan to say it in English: Mr. Gorbachev, open this gate.

Despite Reagan's instructions, Robinson had left out the call to tear down the Wall. "What did you do that for?" Dolan asked. Robinson explained that to Germans, the Brandenburg Gate, not the Wall, was the more resonant symbol of division. Dolan shook his head. In his handwritten markup of the draft, next to "Mr. Gorbachev, open this gate," Dolan scrawled the words *"Tear down this Wall."* The next day, Robinson submitted another draft incorporating Dolan's suggestions. This time he took out the German line about opening the Brandenburg Gate and replaced it with "tear down this Wall"—but in German. *Herr Gorbachev, reissen Sie diese Mauer neider.*

Dolan told Robinson he was pleased with the revisions. "He thought it excellent," Peter wrote in his journal. "I feel confident about it now." But he knew the speech had a long way to go. "May it survive circulation," he wrote.

Every speech at the White House went through extensive editing. During Reagan's second term, the speechwriters' access to the president was curtailed by Donald Regan, the imperious chief of staff. Prior to the May 18 meeting, which had been approved by Regan's successor, Howard Baker, the speechwriters had gone months since hearing from the president in person. Reagan himself was doing less and less of his own writing and editing, which gave the senior staff more influence over the content. Major foreign policy addresses, especially those having to do with the Soviet

Union, were scrutinized closely by officials at the State Department and National Security Council for language that might cause diplomatic offense. Few received more attention than the "Remarks on East-West Relations at the Brandenburg Gate."

Reagan's aides had grown particularly sensitive about how to address Gorbachev. Many still viewed the Soviet leader with skepticism, but they knew Reagan had developed a bond with Gorbachev and saw him as a new kind of Soviet leader. Shultz, in particular, believed Reagan's old, confrontational rhetoric was out of step with the times. In early 1987, chief of staff Regan had met with the speechwriters and told them the president wanted them to go easier on Gorbachev. "We said, 'Oh, *sure*,'" Peter Robinson recalls. "It's not the president, it's you. *You* want us to go easier on Gorbachev." A week later, Regan surprised Robinson and the others by bringing them into the Oval Office. "Reagan didn't quite put it as bluntly as, 'I'd like you to ease up on Gorbachev.' But he did say, 'Well, this fella is different and I think he wants to get out of Afghanistan.'" Robinson says with a laugh, "I do remember walking out of there and thinking that my entire view of the universe had to be readjusted. Ronald Reagan had gone soft on communism."

The National Security Council's initial reaction to the Berlin speech was relatively mild. A one-page memo sent to the speechwriters on May 21 suggested a few cuts and thematic changes. It emphasizes the need to promote a "positive vision" for the future of Germany. It recommends that the speech include language from Kornblum's draft, which had been forwarded to the speechwriting office three weeks earlier. The challenge to Gorbachev is not mentioned; in fact the NSC indicates its agreement that "It's time for the Wall to come down." But objections came from other quarters. On May 27, the U.S. embassy in Bonn sent the State Department its five-page response to the White House draft. The speech was too confrontational, the embassy said. It needed to take into account the popularity of Gorbachev among Germans. "Germans are impatient for movement. They hope Gorbachev can make it possible." West German officials had requested "that there be no harsh polemics against the Soviet Union. . . . A large number of Germans believe that progress will be possible only if we hold back on direct condemnation during this period of change." The biggest problem with the speech was that "many Berliners will see the tone of the current White House draft as being confrontational and detrimental to the progress they deeply desire."

At the State Department, anxiety about the speech started to rise. On May 27, Rozanne Ridgway, one of Shultz's closest aides, sent a confidential memo to Colin Powell, who had given her a copy of the speechwriters' draft. Ridgway ticked off a litany of concerns: the draft "includes too many German phrases . . . lengthier statements tend to be confusing to a German crowd"; the speech condemned the East German regime "too harshly," given that Berliners "are actively trying to play down the image of their city being . . . under siege from the East"; Robinson had Reagan calling for the 1992 Olympic Games to be held in Berlin, when they'd already been awarded to Barcelona. And Ridgway thought the challenge to Gorbachev sounded, at the least, awkward. "The draft invites Gorbachev to come to Berlin if he seeks peace, prosperity and liberalization. This may ring somewhat contrived in view of the fact that Gorbachev will have been in East Berlin two weeks prior to the President's visit."

After receiving Ridgway's memo, Powell called Griscom to urge him to hold off on giving the speech to the president. The NSC wanted to do its own rewrite. "We do not concur with the speech being forwarded to the President in its current form," reads one memo from the NSC. The official assigned to handle revisions on the speech was Peter Rodman, a smart, lanky foreign policy veteran who had been a top aide to Henry Kissinger. Rodman had earlier talked the speechwriters through the concrete policy ideas the State Department wanted Reagan to emphasize. Robinson's draft had neglected nearly all of them. What happened? Rodman called Dolan on May 27 to complain. The speech could not go to the president in its present form, he said. Working with two Europe specialists at the NSC, Fritz Ermarth and Nelson Ledsky, Rodman took a hatchet to Robinson's draft, correcting some of his German quotations and eliminating others (the Marlene Dietrich song "is about *abandonment* of Berlin"), crossing out entire pages of text and replacing them with new ones. The challenge to Gorbachev as Robinson wrote it was removed; instead Rodman's draft read, "Twenty-six years after the Wall was built, it's time for that Wall to come down."

On May 28, Robinson went for a thirty-minute run, then spent "all day on Berlin." He put in some of Rodman's changes, but ignored the NSC's proposed passive voice phrasing on the Wall. The new version went back to the NSC the next day. Rodman's markup was less extensive, though like Ridgway he still found the direct address to Gorbachev grating. Gorbachev will have just been there; did it really make sense to call on him to come back? "This device seems silly, even as edited," he wrote. At the end of the line "Come here, to this gate," he suggested adding, "not to a plush conference hall down the road." He questioned why the challenge to open the Brandenburg Gate was still in German, but the bit about tearing down the Wall was in English.

"There was an unusual amount of tension," Rodman said, reflecting two decades later on the debates over the speech. "I don't remember other speeches where there was this much, you know, pulling and pushing on the content." Of his own role, Rodman joked, "I'm one of the bad guys." In a series of memos to Powell, Rodman could barely contain his frustration with the speechwriters. "We tried every tactic," he wrote. "We offered general guidance, and general suggestions in the margins; we offered detailed rewrites. Neither tactic worked." In his next note Rodman informs Powell that he had "given up on any further major improvements."

The Brandenburg Gate address "is better than before, but the staff is still unanimous that it's a mediocre speech and a missed opportunity."

Powell had doubts of his own. The three-star general had worked for Reagan's defense secretary, Caspar Weinberger, before moving to Frankfurt, Germany, as the head of the Army's V Corps. Shortly before his fiftieth birthday, he returned to the White House as Carlucci's deputy. Though he had little personal investment in the Berlin speech, Powell believed his staff's misgivings were being overlooked. Robinson remembers being summoned to Tom Griscom's windowless office and finding Powell waiting for him. Powell made a forceful case for the changes his staff had requested. "It was very tense," Robinson says. "He raised his voice. And then I also recall a feeling of surprise that I got right back in his face." Powell continued to lobby for changes. The closer it got to the day of the speech, the more directly Powell got involved. At one point he sent over additional revisions to Griscom, attached with a handwritten note: "Please call me and let me explain the rationale page by page before you act on the suggestions."

Robinson's journal records that he rewrote the speech at least seven times after turning in the initial draft to Dolan. The tug-of-war had left him exhausted and disheartened. Robinson's original draft had been subjected to dozens, even hundreds, of cuts, adds, corrections, and changes. And yet the central "animating idea"— Reagan calling on Gorbachev to tear down the Wall—had survived. Griscom, it turns out, had kept the president informed of the running objections to the speech. "I kept going back just to make sure and reconfirm—here's what we're talking about saying, and are you still comfortable saying it?" Griscom says. "And I got to hear him deliver the line several times in advance sitting in the Oval Office. You knew that if this stayed in the speech, if he ever stood up in front of that gate in Berlin, this had the potential of being a very powerful line."

Still, not everyone was convinced. Just days before the president left for Europe, Griscom got a call from chief of staff Howard Baker, for whom he had worked when Baker was Senate majority leader. Baker told Griscom he thought the challenge to Gorbachev was unrealistic. It would never happen. It was un-presidential. Would Griscom mind coming down to his office to discuss it? When Griscom walked in, Baker had another person in his office: George Shultz. "Tommy," Baker said, "why don't you tell him why this needs to be in the speech?" Griscom said he thought the line would be memorable; he believed it was something Reagan wanted to say. Shultz glared at him. "Young man, you may set back all the progress we've made in U.S.-Soviet relations." Griscom had been in the White House less than six months. "Mr. Secretary, I will never have the experience and background you've got," he said. "But what I can tell you is I think it's right."

Shultz disputes Griscom's version of events. "I would not have objected to that line," he says now. "I would have applauded that line, because I said similar things myself." He continues, "There was always this feeling that if things are going well, that is, we were making progress with Gorbachev, don't do something provocative. There are people who have that attitude. And there are some good arguments for it. But I never felt that way and neither did President Reagan." Whatever the case, the crucial point is that, given numerous opportunities to alter, revise, or reconsider making the challenge to Gorbachev in Berlin, Reagan himself never showed any inclination to do so. He didn't agonize over it. Perhaps he relied on his intuition, an old actor's sixth sense for the killer line. But there may be another, simpler explanation: he thought it would work. Reagan believed in reaching out to Gorbachev, but always in the interest of pushing the Soviet leader to keep pursuing change. "It was kind of presumptuous of the bureaucrats to say, 'Oh, this is going to annoy Gorbachev,' or negatively affect our relationship with him," Peter Rodman said before his death in 2008. "Reagan had no hesitation. He knew Gorbachev. I think the intuition of Reagan was that Gorbachev was somebody who knew something was wrong with the Soviet system. So maybe he had noticed a certain moral awareness on Gorbachev's part and was pushing at it."

On the evening of June 1, Dolan delivered the latest version of the Berlin speech to the Oval Office. The cover letter said, "Please find attached your Brandenburg remarks. There are several German phrases for which we will provide phonetics. Please let us know if you feel they present a problem." Reagan read the speech and put his initials "RR" on the upper-right-hand corner. He made no other markings on it.

How closely Reagan reviewed the speech is anyone's guess. He managed to overlook at least one glaring flaw in the text—the line "Mr. Gorbachev, open this gate" was still in German. Given his lack of interest in programmatic details, he may barely have glanced at the policy initiatives on Berlin the State Department hoped would make the most news. But then, Reagan already knew what he really wanted to say. Five days before he set off for Europe, Reagan gave a group interview to six foreign television journalists at the White House. "Mr. President," one questioner said, "let me have one question on Berlin. You will be in Berlin. What are you going to tell Germans in East and West, and what are you going to achieve there?"

"Well," Reagan replied, "I think I'm going to express the belief that all of us have: that there should be a reunited Germany and that the Wall should come down."

7. THE WALL MUST GO

The presidential delegation left for Europe at 9 A.M. on June 3. Departing from the South Lawn of the White House that morning, the Reagans were sent off by a crowd of staffers and students from nearby James Madison High School, who gave the president an American flag pin for his lapel. The Marine Band played "Hail to the Chief." Though he had by now visited more than twenty foreign countries as president, Reagan retained an almost boyish fascination with the experience of crossing time zones, of flying in daylight to a place where it was already dark. Reagan was served breakfast and dinner on the flight to Venice, which lasted eight hours and twenty minutes. As he reclined in State Room 1, the front right cabin of Air Force One, Reagan evidently spent time gazing out at the bright skies. "At 9:42 Venice time it was still daylight," he recorded in his diary. "Where [we] were it was 7:42 & 3:42 in Washington."

At the back of the plane, Carlucci and Marlin Fitzwater, the press secretary, briefed the reporters traveling with the president. A pool of fourteen journalists was aboard Air Force One, with another two hundred flying over in a separate press plane. The pool asked about the appointment of Alan Greenspan to replace Paul Volcker as chairman of the Federal Reserve, the Iranian government's threats against U.S. ships in the Persian Gulf, and the ongoing arms control talks with the Soviets. The president's upcoming speech in Berlin never came up. A reporter asked Carlucci about Reagan's mood. "Very upbeat," Carlucci said. "He's looking forward to the challenge."

Overseas travel was taxing for Reagan. The break from routine, the jet lag and jam-packed itineraries, often left him worn out and disoriented. On a visit to Brazil early in his presidency, he gave a toast saying how wonderful it was to be in Bolivia. (The next day a Brazilian in São Paolo unfurled a banner along the route of the presidential motorcade. THE PEOPLE OF BOLIVIA WELCOME THE PRESIDENT OF CANADA. "Reagan thought it was funny as hell," Shultz says.) He fell asleep at inopportune times, as during his audience with John Paul II in the papal library in 1982 or while listening to a Gorbachev toast at the Moscow summit in 1988. Once he dozed off at a meeting with Japanese officials in London. When it was over, he shook hands with his Japanese interpreter. "Well, Mr. Foreign Minister, it sure has been a pleasure," he said.

At the insistence of Michael Deaver and the first lady, Reagan's staff sought to minimize the potential for such gaffes. They shielded the president from reporters and scheduled several days of rest before any significant meetings or photo ops. His trip to Europe followed that script. Upon arriving in Venice the Reagans were taken to Condulmer, a three-hundred-year-old villa outside the city that had been turned into a hotel with a swimming pool and eighteen-hole golf course. "Very beautiful but not quite as convenient as [the] Hilton," Reagan observed. A handcrafted bed used by the Reagans during an earlier European trip had been flown in from Lisbon. Though he admired the opulent setting, Reagan would have preferred one with basic amenities. "I have to say these grand old buildings are beautiful, magnificent with their marble floors, tapestries, & paintings—and inconvenient. This last word has to do with bathrooms & showers & no place to put your razor, toothbrush etc."

For the next two days, Reagan read briefing books for the G-7 summit, took walks in the gardens of the villa, suntanned by the pool, and watched John Wayne and Laurel and Hardy movies. On June 5, "a beautiful, sun shiny day," he sat down with Carlucci and Ken Duberstein, the deputy chief of staff. Duberstein brought up Reagan's speech at the Berlin Wall. Before leaving Washington, Duberstein had taken a call from George Shultz, who reiterated the State Department's objections to the line in the speech challenging Gorbachev to tear down the Wall. "He didn't ask me for ten minutes on the president's calendar to object to the line," Duberstein later said. "He asked me to convey his concern. Which, as any savvy chief of staff knows, meant, 'It's all on your shoulders, Duberstein. If it screws up it's yours.'" Duberstein relayed Shultz's message and gave Reagan a copy of the speech, asking him to reread the passage on the Wall. Reagan looked at Duberstein. "What do you think?" he asked. "I think it's a hell of a line," Duberstein replied, "but you're the president and you get to decide." There was a twinkle in Reagan's eye. "I think we'll leave it in," he said.

The speech wasn't a finished product yet. In Washington, the NSC and the speechwriters continued to trade revisions. A June 4 markup by the NSC's Peter Rodman featured extensive changes. This time he sought to excise the last three pages of the speech—including Robinson's peroration about the love that kept West Berliners in the city and the anecdote about the television tower at Alexanderplatz. The passage contained too many lines referring to the East German government as "totalitarian" and "brutish," Rodman said. "West Germans do NOT want to see East Germans insulted," he wrote in the margins. He inserted a shorter, substitute ending that did not refer to the East German regime. When Robinson received Rodman's latest revisions, he sent a memo to Dolan, who was with Reagan in Italy. "I leave it to you to decide what to do about Peter Rodman's sixth rewrite. For myself, I reject it completely."

Other problems remained. Robinson's researchers had found that the story about the East Germans' removing a cross from the sculpture atop the Brandenburg Gate was false; Robinson told Dolan that would have to come out. And the speech still contained several long German phrases that sounded awkward. "Mr. Gorbachev, open this gate" still read *Herr Gorbachev, machen Sie dieses Tor auf.* "This line that got repeated five thousand times the week of Ronald Reagan's funeral—we had it right under our noses and we were still fumbling around with it," Robinson says. "I was going back and forth about what should be in German and what should be in English. You would have a German audience in front of him and an American audience watching on television. How much English would the Germans understand? How many German phrases do you want to put in for that audience?"

The NSC believed there were still too many. Rodman suggested putting "open this gate" back into English, but Robinson refused. On June 8, just four days before the speech, the White House faxed the latest version to the Cipriani hotel in Venice, where most of the staff and traveling press were staying. The president would soon be getting the final text. A draft dated June 8, which was displayed in the rotunda of the Ronald Reagan Presidential Library on the twentieth anniversary of the speech, shows what appear to be the final written revisions made to the "Remarks on East-West Relations at the Brandenburg Gate." There's no handwriting on the draft, just black lines drawn through three German phrases: *Freiheit ist der Sieger* ("Freedom is the victor"); *Die Mauer kahn Freiheit nicht zuruckhalen* ("The Wall cannot withstand freedom"); and *Herr Gorbachev, machen Sie dieses Tor auf* ("Mr. Gorbachev, open this gate"). Based solely on the physical document, it is impossible to determine the hand behind those markings. But they most likely would have been made by an official, such as National Security Adviser Carlucci, who was traveling with the president and had the authority to overrule the speechwriters.

The speech that finally emerged from the interagency brawl bore only passing resemblance to the one Peter Robinson first drafted in mid-May. It was stronger in many ways. The main challenge to Gorbachev had been sharpened and rephrased entirely in English. Many of Robinson's more lyrical lines survived ("Standing before the Brandenburg Gate, every man is a German, separated from his fellow men. Every man is a Berliner, forced to look upon a scar."), but so did some composed by Rodman and the NSC ("East and West do not mistrust each other because we are armed. We are armed because we mistrust each other."). Read today, the weakest section is the one devoted to the State Department's Berlin initiative, the details of which are now lost in the mists of history. The speech ends with a typically Reaganesque passage, in which he quotes a phrase spray-painted on the Wall that he claims to have just seen: THIS WALL WILL FALL. BELIEFS BECOME REALITY (since the line was written weeks before Reagan stepped foot in Berlin, the claim is dubious). "Yes, across Europe this Wall will fall," the speech concludes. "For it cannot withstand faith; it cannot withstand truth. The Wall cannot withstand freedom."

As a written piece of oratory, "Remarks on East-West Relations at the Brandenburg Gate" does not rank as the most eloquent of Reagan's career. His address at Westminster had more historical sweep, "The Boys of Pointe du Hoc" speech more lyricism, the tribute to the crew of the Challenger more emotional resonance. All writers complain that the editing process inevitably muddles the clarity of their prose; the final product is never as good as the original. Peter Robinson was understandably despondent over the number of times he had to rewrite the Berlin Wall speech. And yet its most memorable lines—the ones that would prove to be the most enduring of Reagan's presidency—might have lost their rhetorical power without the last-minute changes made by other members of Reagan's staff. As the main writer of the speech, Robinson ultimately deserves the lion's share of the credit for the language and content of the Berlin Wall address. It does not diminish the weight of his accomplishment to say that many others helped make it better.

In the days leading up to his arrival in Berlin, Reagan met with two allies in his crusade against communism. The first was Pope John Paul II. Reagan and the pope first met in Rome in 1982, bonding over their common fates: both had survived assassination attempts that instilled in them a determination to fulfill their God-given missions in life. Both loathed the suppression of religion in the communist world. In the early 1980s, after the Soviet-backed government in the pope's native Poland imposed martial law, Reagan had phoned the pope to pledge the U.S.'s support for the anti-communist opposition and its leader, Lech Walesa. Quietly encouraged by the pope, the Polish clergy became a crucial bulwark to the anti-communist Solidarity movement. In the broadest sense, both Reagan and John Paul II believed that, if unleashed, the moral power of the faithful could one day overcome the godlessness of totalitarianism. "I have had a feeling," Reagan wrote to a friend early in his presidency, "that religion may very well turn out to be the Soviets' Achilles heel."

Reagan's meeting with the pope in Rome on June 6 lasted just under an hour. "As best I could" Reagan gave the pontiff an update on the progress of arms control talks in Geneva, the war in Nicaragua, and his assessment of Gorbachev. The pope urged Reagan to end the arms race. Doing so would free up resources to feed the world's poor, he said. After the meeting Reagan delivered a short speech, based on the ideas he had outlined to Josh Gilder in the Oval Office meeting three weeks earlier. He did not mention Gorbachev by name, but his remarks were aimed as much at an audience in the Kremlin as at the Vatican. "Perhaps it's not too much to hope that true change will come to all countries that now deny or hinder the freedom to worship God," he said. "Perhaps we'll see that change comes through the reemergence of faith, through the irresistible power of a religious renewal." At the time, Reagan's words sounded bold even to the pope, who was about to make his third visit to Poland and who was at pains not to offend its leaders. But throughout Eastern Europe and the Soviet Union, religious dissidents would indeed play a crucial role in bringing about communism's collapse. Like the address Reagan would give in Berlin, his remarks at the Vatican, read now, have an element of prophecy.

Two days later Reagan joined his staff at the Cipriani hotel, on Giudecca Island, for the start of the G-7 summit. Margaret Thatcher waited there to see him. At sixty-one, Thatcher was at the height of her popularity in Britain, two days away from a landslide reelection. Though she was Reagan's closest friend among world leaders, Thatcher had long viewed his talk about abolishing nuclear weapons as hopelessly naive. "From time to time he would come out with his talk about a 'world without nuclear weapons,'" she later said. "It is a world I cannot foresee because there have always been evil people in the world." And while she had been the first to recognize, as early as 1984, that Gorbachev was a "man we can do business with," she was more skeptical than Reagan about the possibility for change behind the Iron Curtain. In March 1987, she told the House of Commons, "The Berlin Wall is the most visible sign of the way in which borders operate round a Communist society. It will be a long time, if indeed it ever happens, before people there enjoy the freedom we enjoy." In Venice, she pressed Reagan on the "zero-zero" arms reduction proposal with the Soviets, which would eliminate all short-range and tactical nuclear weapons in Europe. Echoing American conservatives, she argued that such a deal would leave Western Europe vulnerable to an attack by the Soviets, who retained conventional military superiority over NATO. At dinner on June 8, Thatcher argued past midnight with German chancellor Kohl, who had come out in favor of the zero-zero approach.

In Reagan's words, "She says no & I had to differ with her." He woke up at seven the next morning to meet with Thatcher again. He assured the prime minister he wouldn't be outmaneuvered by Gorbachev. That seemed to satisfy Thatcher. "We are on the same wavelength," Reagan later wrote.

Still, Reagan did not give a good performance in Venice. He liked the pageantry of these events, the foreign honor guards and elaborate dinners, but had little interest in the plenary sessions and position papers that are the nuts-and-bolts work of economic summits. His lack of engagement showed. Diplomats at the summit told reporters that Reagan seemed distracted and preoccupied. When his counterparts challenged him about the U.S.'s soaring budget deficit, he let Shultz and Treasury Secretary James Baker do the talking. Television cameras caught Shultz nudging him to stay awake during the reading of the final communiqué. Even in one-on-one meetings with the other G-7 leaders, Reagan resorted to reading prepared lines off his index cards. Only when the subject turned to Gorbachev did he seem his usual, animated self.

On June 11, the last day of the summit, Reagan took questions from the traveling press. NBC's Andrea Mitchell asked Reagan why Europeans liked Gorbachev more than him. "Maybe all of you could have helped change that if you worked a little harder at it," Reagan said laughing, but then continued, "Maybe because it's so unusual. This is the first Soviet leader, in my memory, that has ever advocated actually eliminating weapons already built and in place." Mitchell pressed Reagan about whether he trusted Gorbachev, if he believed the Soviet leader "is a man of peace and that he does want to sincerely reduce weapons and that a verifiable treaty can be reached?" Aware of how conservatives at home would respond, Reagan chose his words carefully, saying that Gorbachev was "a personable gentleman." But he also offered an assessment of Gorbachev that was more keenly astute than those made by some of the experts advising him. "I've had meetings with him. And I do believe he is faced with an economic problem in his own country that has been aggravated by the military buildup and all. And I believe he has some pretty practical reasons for why he would like to see a successful outcome." Reagan said he thought the arms race could be brought to an end. "We believe," he told Mitchell, "that we have a good chance of bringing about the beginning of reducing and eliminating nuclear weapons."

As gatherings of world leaders often do, the Venice summit attracted media attention vastly out of proportion to its actual importance. The real news was happening elsewhere. The day after Reagan met the pope in Rome, an anonymous caller claiming to be from a radical Palestinian group phoned the office of an Italian news agency in Beirut. He warned of attacks against Italian interests "everywhere" because of Reagan's presence in Venice. On the morning of June 9, two explosive devices fired from a construction site in downtown Rome landed in a reflecting pool in front of the British embassy. Not long after, a Ford Escort containing four pounds of explosives detonated on a street next to the U.S. embassy; at about the same time, two devices fired from a nearby hotel landed in the garden of the embassy, cracking windows and scarring the building's facade. In Venice, Reagan was briefed on the bombings, which put security forces on alert for possible threats against the dignitaries. In his diary Reagan recorded that a mine floating in a nearby canal was seized and detonated. It turned out to be an old water heater.

Even more newsworthy events were unfolding in the president's next destination, Berlin. As part of the celebration of the city's 750th birthday, West Berlin played host to a three-day music festival featuring David Bowie, Phil Collins, and Eurythmics. The concert was held in the park in front of the Reichstag, well within earshot of the Brandenburg Gate and the eastern side of the Berlin Wall. On the night of June 6, a few hundred young East Germans, some who had traveled from other parts of the country for the event, congregated at a section of the Wall near the Brandenburg Gate, hoping to listen to the concert. They were met by a cordon of police who forced the youths back from the border area. According to the Stasi's confidential report on the incident, the crowd heckled the police, but no violence broke out. The next night a bigger crowd, numbering close to one thousand, showed up. The police locked arms in front of the Wall. The tension rose. The crowd chanted, "The Wall must go!" The Stasi file on the incident reports the police made thirty-four arrests. "Nobody was injured, nothing was damaged," the report said.

The government's businesslike tone belies how unexpected the protests were. As the East German government increased the surveillance of its citizens' lives, large-scale demonstrations of any kind had become rare. East German newspapers did not report the disturbances of June 6 and June 7. But accounts had already spread among young activists in East Berlin trying to fight the system. "We decided we had to go there the next night," says Christian Halbrock, at the time a member of a small church-based opposition group. "If there was a clash you wanted to be able to say to your friends, 'I was there.'" Halbrock was in his early twenties, the son of a religious family who grew up listening to Western radio and music. Because he was not a member of the Communist Party, the government barred him from taking the university entrance exams; instead he did various apprenticeships and moved to East Berlin. He got a ten-hour-a-week job at a church bookstore. In the evenings he helped research and write pamphlets critical of the government. The Wall had sundered his ties to members of his family. His older brother lived in West Berlin, and Christian was unable to visit him. "There were people in East Germany of my generation who felt that enough was enough," he says. "Our parents had made too many compromises. We decided we needed to take more action against the system."

Halbrock and his friends went to the Wall on June 8, the last night of the concert at the Reichstag. East German police had parked trucks near the Wall and kept the engines running, to ensure that the music from the other side was inaudible. The crowd soon swelled to more than two thousand. According to a Security Ministry report, they taunted the police with cries of "Pig," "Russians Out," and "Wall Down." At one point some in the crowd started chanting "Gorby! Gorby!" "The protest was in front of the Soviet embassy," Halbrock recalls. "We thought the police wouldn't dare to beat someone yelling 'Gorby' because then they'd be beating someone supporting the Soviet Union." When the lightly armed police tried to push them back, the crowd began throwing rocks and bottles. The police called for reinforcements from the government's security services, who stormed into the crowd, pulling demonstrators behind police lines and beating them brutally. At least 120 were arrested; those who ended up in jail were fined for participating in the protests. Many said they were tortured. An East German witness later claimed that two protesters were killed when a police car ran over them. The clashes lasted until 1:25 A.M. The Stasi report again tried to downplay them. "Nobody was injured, nothing damaged," the report said.

However brief, the open-air concert protests represented a turning point in the history of the GDR. Not since the labor revolt of 1953 had the government confronted such an open display of public hostility. The clashes highlighted "the continued unacceptability of the Wall for the East German population and of the GDR regime which needs to hide behind it," U.S. ambassador to West Germany Richard Burt wrote in a confidential cable to Shultz and Carlucci. Burt wrote that "there is no serious threat to the East German regime," but said the violence meant that Reagan's speech "will have even greater resonance" than it might otherwise have had. "On the other hand the disturbances have heightened sensitivities among Germans on both sides of the divide and will mean that the President's remarks, especially on the subject of the Wall, will be subjected to especially close scrutiny." Burt suggested that the speech be reviewed again "to ensure that it strikes the right balance."

The outbreak of violence at the Wall shook the East German regime. To the communists, Reagan's visit was suddenly seen as a destabilizing event, something that could stir up emotions and spark more embarrassing demonstrations against their rule. The Stasi files show that the government believed the open-air protests had been incited by West German agents, "part of an aggressive campaign against the Wall that is apparently connected to the appearance of US President Reagan on June 12th 87." A June 9 memo predicted that Reagan's speech would include "insulting and inflammatory comments against the GDR." The state police worried that Reagan's speech could encourage anti-government demonstrations that would receive publicity from opposition figures and "journalists from non-socialist countries." It urged security officials to seal all borders leading into West Berlin and prevent "gatherings close to the border, especially at the Brandenburg Gate."

A more detailed set of orders from Erich Honecker, the East German leader, spelled out security measures to be carried out during the speech. They are a revealing glimpse at the regime's insecurity, anti-Western hostility, and paranoia. Anyone attempting to go near the border would be detained indefinitely. Foreign journalists were banned from interviewing East Berliners. Loudspeakers would be positioned near the Brandenburg Gate. If Reagan's speech were audible on the eastern side of the Wall, the East Germans would drown him out.

As always, what most concerned the authorities were the activities of their own citizens. On June 10, a group of intellectuals met in Gerd Poppe's apartment, at 28 Rykestrasse in Prenzlauer Berg. They were joined by an American representative of the Helsinki Watch Committee, a human rights group. They discussed the status of human rights in East Germany and the growth of pro-democracy movements in Poland and Czechoslovakia. The next day Poppe and his colleagues gathered at the apartment of Werner Fischer, a member of Poppe's Initiative for Peace and Human Rights. They talked about the recent violence at the Wall and developed a plan to publish eyewitness testimonials about acts of police brutality there.

"People who are active in the sense of a political underground in the capital of the GDR," a report by the Stasi said, "did not display a synchronized or coordinated reaction or activities in connection with the Reagan visit." During the June 10 meeting in Poppe's apartment, "the subject did not come up." There was only one way the regime could have known that: one of Poppe's friends was a Stasi informer. For Werner Fischer, the truth was even more shattering. Years after the Wall came down, Fischer would learn he had been informed on by his own mother.

On the eve of Reagan's visit, anxiety was rising in West Berlin too. City officials had tried to dissuade the administration from staging Reagan's speech at the Brandenburg Gate, but because of Berlin's special status, the U.S. retained ultimate authority over security matters. Now the Germans wanted to limit the number of people who could attend it. They told John Kornblum, the U.S.'s highest-ranking official in Berlin, that the site near the Gate could accommodate only fifteen thousand people. The White House wanted forty thousand. Running security checks on that many people was impossible, the Germans said. But Kornblum and his team believed they could do it. The families of American diplomats and soldiers stationed in Berlin would account for ten thousand spots. The rest could be drawn from the employee lists of big multinational companies with offices in Berlin, like BMW, Siemens, and Ford. "We went to all these big companies and said, 'If you could invite for us all the people off of your employee lists, we will guarantee they can come to the President's speech,'" Kornblum says. "They were thrilled to do this. They thought it was a great idea. And then we said to the police, 'We're doing this. You load your security files in here and we're going to check them.'" Running the names through mid-1980s-era PCs took Kornblum's staff nearly four days. When they were done some forty thousand people had been cleared to see the American president.

Reagan's security detail wasn't convinced he was safe. The Secret Service believed that the site chosen by the advance team would leave the president exposed to snipers. "They were terribly afraid that some East German would shoot President Reagan while he was delivering his speech," says Leopold-Bill von Bredow, the chief of protocol in West Berlin. Bredow argued that the risk of an assassination attempt was remote, given how tightly the East Germans controlled their people; besides, the Russians, who still had authority over East Berlin, would never let it happen. That didn't sway the Secret Service, which ordered that a fifteen-foot-high bulletproof wall be erected behind the podium where the president would speak. But that presented another problem. The audience in Berlin would be able to see the Wall as Reagan spoke, but Americans watching on TV would not. The advance team pushed back. "We said, 'Well, that totally defeats our purpose,'" says James Hooley, the head of the advance office. A compromise was reached: the planners decided to remove the portion of the armored screen directly behind the presidential lectern and replace it with bullet-proof glass. Now, when Reagan gave his speech, a section of the Wall would be visible behind him.

The Reagan team's preoccupation with security stemmed more from the 1981 assassination attempt than an expectation that Reagan would be targeted from the other side of the Wall. But concern for the president's safety was not altogether misplaced. In addition to the protective screen behind the speaker's dais, the Secret Service constructed a bulletproof enclosure around the balcony on the

Reichstag from which Reagan would look into East Berlin. "Look, nothing's going to happen here," Kornblum recalls telling Reagan's security men. Later Kornblum realized that twenty feet from the Reichstag, the East Germans had set up an eavesdropping station packed with spies. "If somebody had wanted to do something—maybe not even on orders, but just because he was a bastard—it would have been easy enough to do it," Kornblum says now.

While the White House worried about threats from the East, German officials fretted about what leftists in the West might try to do to disrupt the Reagan visit. Just days after the clashes between police and demonstrators near the Wall in East Berlin, violence broke out in West Berlin. For more than a month, local anarchist groups had waged running street battles with police, smashing windows and torching storefronts. The unrest was centered in Kreuzberg, a West Berlin neighborhood populated by artists, musicians, immigrants, and punks. On June 11, an anti-Reagan demonstration down the Kurfürstendamm, the main shopping district in West Berlin, drew some thirty thousand protesters. The march remained peaceful until a group of two thousand anarchists, wearing black masks and positioned in the middle of the crowd, began throwing steel balls, bottles, and Molotov cocktails hidden in planters along the route. They set fire to construction sites and smashed store windows. The West Berlin police responded with tear gas. In Kreuzberg, the riot lasted into the early morning hours, leaving dozens of policemen injured and causing hundreds of thousands of dollars in damage. Undercover police who infiltrated the demonstration learned that the militants intended to stage another major disturbance during Reagan's visit the next day. They wanted to "flatten" the Kurfürstendamm. "We in Berlin love traditions," wrote one commentator in the left-wing newspaper *Tageszeitung*. "And when Ronald Reagan comes, you demonstrate."

Wrapping up the G-7 meeting in Venice, Reagan would have been only vaguely aware of the tumult taking place on both sides of the Berlin Wall. Reports of the violence overnight in West Berlin did not appear in the newspapers until after he arrived there. On June 11, he spent his last day in Venice, concluding the summit with a news conference. "Thank Heaven it turned out to be a good one," he wrote. He posed for photographs with the naval personnel who had guided him through the Venetian canals. The president walked around the grounds of the Cipriani a final time, had dinner with the first lady in their suite, and went to bed early. He was ready to leave. "Tomorrow Berlin Bonn & then home," he wrote that night.

All across Berlin there was a quiet scramble to prepare. Near the Wall, the final pieces of bulletproof glass were set in place behind the speaker's podium. Workers draped bunting of black, red, and gold—the colors of the West German flag—over the front of the dais. At least ten thousand policemen headed onto the streets, reinforced by 1,100 officers from other parts of West Germany, the biggest police mobilization in the city's history. Before dawn, police in East Berlin blocked pedestrian areas and set up barricades on the Unter den Linden to prevent anyone from trying to venture near the Berlin Wall. And a team of East German commandos positioned themselves atop the Brandenburg Gate, ready to watch Reagan's every move.

8. THE SIGN OF THE CROSS

Germany crawled with Russian spies. At the height of the Cold War, the number of KGB agents living in East Germany ran into the thousands. With the help of the Stasi, the KGB identified East Germans with credible "legends," or cover stories, who were willing to help the USSR steal military secrets but wouldn't arouse suspicion in the West. Hundreds of East German professors, journalists, scientists, and engineers were recruited. One former KGB agent, posted in the East German city of Dresden, later acknowledged that "we were interested in any information about the 'main opponent,' as we called them, and the main opponent was considered NATO." This thirty-two-year-old agent lived with his wife and two small children in a service apartment that housed families of Russian and German spies. Compared to the bread lines and shortages that were typical of life in Russia, East Germany seemed like a land of plenty. The KGB man drove a better car than the locals, which the family used for weekend trips to Saxony. "There was always plenty of everything," he later said, including some of the best beer in East Germany, which he drank straight from the keg. Eating lunch at home every day, he put on twenty pounds. Such was life as a secret agent for Vladimir Vladimirovich Putin.

The Soviets were most active in Berlin. As Reagan's visit neared, they were consumed with muzzling any show of interest in the speech among the population in East Berlin. The KGB believed such scenes could embarrass the Kremlin. A few weeks earlier, a group of eleven exchange students from Moscow State University had arrived in Berlin. One of them was Svetlana Savranskaya, a blond, ambitious twenty-one-year-old who was studying contemporary history, with a focus on the United States. Savranskaya had been preparing for her wedding in July when she was asked by university administrators if she was interested in spending a few weeks in Berlin. She didn't speak any German, but the administrators said she fit the other criteria: she was "politically acceptable" and had a spotless academic record. Svetlana jumped at the opportunity. Once in Berlin, she visited every museum and took in a performance of the ballet *Spartacus*. "The dancers wore almost nothing!" she recalls. "It was very shocking, but not for the Germans." She engaged East German students, many of whom spoke Russian, in long discussions about history, politics, and the prospects for reform in the socialist bloc—things she wouldn't dream of doing back in the USSR. There were limits, however. The Russian students were to avoid talking to Westerners. If they saw an American soldier on the streets, they were not to make contact of any kind with him. "And we were warned to not even come close to the Wall."

In early June, she heard about Reagan's visit from her German friends. Some excitedly talked about going to the Unter den Linden, near the Brandenburg Gate, to try to hear the president's speech. None of Svetlana's Russian classmates showed any interest, but she decided she would go anyway. The night before Reagan's speech, the administrator accompanying Svetlana's group pulled the students aside. "You may know about this event happening tomorrow," he said. "I want you to be clear—no one should be there, not even close. You represent Moscow State University. It will be an international scandal if you are seen there. So don't even think about it."

Svetlana stayed up late that night, full of nervous energy. "I was so focused on being there, but I was also scared," she says. She ditched her Soviet-style clothes and borrowed a denim jacket from a German friend, to help her blend into the crowd. On the morning of June 12, she woke up early, left her dorm, and headed for the Brandenburg Gate. She arrived at a spot on the Unter den Linden where a crowd was gathering, two hours before Reagan was scheduled to speak. The East Germans had sealed off the Pariser Platz, the area in front of the Brandenburg Gate, preventing anyone from getting within one thousand yards of the Wall. Two rows of armored police manned the barricades. From a distance Svetlana could barely make out a glass pane, the speaker's platform, the tops of a row of flags. People around her were talking, but Svetlana remained silent. For the next two hours, she stood and waited.

The Reagans awoke at 7:30 A.M. in Venice. Juice and coffee were delivered to their suite. By then most of the three hundred journalists covering the president's trip had arrived at Marco Polo Airport for the press plane's departure to West Berlin. Reagan put on a navy blue pinstriped suit, cufflinks, a red tie with diagonal stripes, and a white pocket square. He made his way to the lobby of the Cipriani, where he thanked and shook hands with the staff. At 9:30 a boat launch took the president and Mrs. Reagan to a helicopter pad at a nearby military school, where they boarded Marine One. The chopper circled over a U.S. Navy vessel, whose sailors stood on deck to salute Reagan, and arrived at the airport fourteen minutes later. At 10:23 A.M., Air Force One took off for Berlin.

On board Reagan ate brunch and reviewed the two speeches he would give that day, the first at the Brandenburg Gate and the second at a "birthday party" for the city to be held at Tempelhof Airport, the military facility that had been the base of operations during the Berlin Airlift. The text of the Brandenburg Gate speech was printed in capital letters on twenty-one four-by-six-inch index cards. As he always did, Reagan marked up the cards with a fountain pen, breaking down the speech into groups of phrases, underlining the words he intended to emphasize, using slashes to mark pauses in the delivery. The overall effect was to establish a meter and cadence for the speech, to give voice to what until then were still just words on paper. When he came across a German phrase, he put it in brackets. Eventually he reached the defining passage, which read:

> GENERAL SECRETARY GORBACHEV, IF YOU
> SEEK PEACE—IF YOU SEEK PROSPERITY FOR
> THE SOVIET UNION AND EASTERN EUROPE—
> IF YOU SEEK LIBERALIZATION: COME HERE,
> TO THIS GATE.
>   MR. GORBACHEV, OPEN THIS GATE.
>   MR. GORBACHEV, TEAR DOWN THIS WALL.

Reagan inserted forward slashes after "peace," "Europe," and "liberalization." He drew lines under both of the lines addressed to Gorbachev.

The battle over the speech was in its final stages. On the morning of the 12th, the NSC sent another draft to the president's aides with suggested changes. Marlin Fitzwater, the White House press secretary, recalls that the president's senior staff gathered one more time in the conference room at the front of the plane. "There were several of us who wanted to raise again this question of why you would want to put in the line 'Tear down this Wall,'" Fitzwater says. "Nobody could point to any solid indication that the Wall was coming down anytime soon, and we were just afraid that it would look a little Pollyannaish." But Reagan put his foot down. "He said definitely no," Fitzwater remembers. "He had thought about it a lot and gone over it a lot and he wanted to leave it in. And that was kind of the end of that."

What Reagan did not know at the time was that the line had already been made public. The night before, the White House had given copies of the speech to reporters traveling with the president, to allow them to write their stories ahead of time. They were under embargo from printing or broadcasting their pieces until 8 A.M. Washington time on Friday, when the president would begin speaking in Berlin. But the *Washington Times* broke the embargo, running a story in its Friday morning edition that quoted from the speech. When she found out about the *Times*'s story, UPI's Helen Thomas, who was on her way to Berlin, filed her prewritten story on the speech. The *Washington Post* decided to pick up Thomas's story and run it on the front page that morning. Thus hours before Reagan had even arrived in West Berlin, readers of the *Post* were greeted with the headline on the front page: REAGAN TO CALL FOR BERLIN WALL'S FALL; GORBACHEV CHALLENGED TO TEAR IT DOWN IN SPEECH SET FOR TODAY.

Few in Washington awoke more mindful of the day's events than Peter Robinson. Dolan had called him the previous night after the speech had been distributed to the press. Dolan was in high spirits, telling Robinson that several reporters had said the speech was one of the best of Reagan's presidency. At lunch that day, Ed Feulner, the president of the Heritage Foundation, had asked Robinson about the speech. Robinson knew this was the most important one he had written. He planned to go for a run that morning and then watch Reagan on television, since the networks had all decided to carry the speech live. "There may be a sense," he wrote in his journal, "that this is a big one."

The Germans remained nervous. When the mayor of West Berlin, Eberhard Diepgen, was briefed on the contents of the speech the day before Reagan arrived, he called American ambassador Richard Burt. The language about tearing down the Wall would provoke the East Germans, Diepgen said. They might try to disrupt Reagan's speech; at the very least, he said, it would damage his efforts to improve relations with the East. Burt pushed back. "I told him that we had looked at this and we had thought it through," Burt says. "I said, 'Mr. Mayor, you have to understand that if Ronald Reagan comes to Berlin, he has got to call for the end of the Berlin Wall. There's no way he can stand there in front of the Wall and not make that statement.'" The speech wasn't up for further discussion.

Air Force One touched down at Tempelhof at 11:42 A.M. It was a mild day in Berlin, the temperature in the sixties and the skies threatening rain. Burt and Bredow, the chief of protocol, climbed the set of stairs leading into the plane to greet Reagan. The first couple had been given a detailed itinerary, which identified each person they would meet during their five hours in Berlin. On any foreign trip, the Reagans studied their scripts closely. Bredow recalls that when he introduced himself to Reagan, the president knew how to pronounce his name. "Whatever they thought at the moment, they were able to give you the feeling that they were really glad to arrive in Berlin," says Bredow. Reagan descended the plane and stepped onto a viewing platform for the arrival ceremony, the U.S. Army band playing "Hail to the Chief" and "The Star-Spangled Banner" as an honor guard fired off a twenty-one-gun salute. From there Reagan's motorcade took him into the city, where he met first with Richard von Weizsäcker, the president of the Federal Republic of Germany, at Bellevue Castle, his official residence in Berlin. Though Weizsäcker's was a ceremonial post, the meeting had some symbolic importance: since West Berlin was not the capital of West Germany, no American president had visited the West German president at his residence there. Having Reagan visit the Bellevue Castle, the White House believed, would underline the U.S.'s commitment to strengthening the city's ties to the West.

An American flag fluttered on the hood of the presidential limousine, which pulled up to the steps of the Reichstag just after 1 P.M. On the way there, Reagan discussed the speech a final time with Ken Duberstein. "The boys at State are going to kill me,"

Duberstein remembers Reagan saying. "But it's the right thing to do." Kohl waited on the red carpet to greet Reagan. As the leaders and their wives posed for photographs, a reporter shouted, "Mr. President, what do you think of the anti-American demonstrations here?" At first Reagan didn't respond, so the reporter shouted again. This time Reagan replied. "The only demonstration I've seen is utmost cordiality and hospitality," he said, smiling. Inside the Reichstag, he shook hands with six elderly German women, the "Rubble Ladies" who had helped to clean up the streets of the city after World War II. "Mr. President," NBC's Chris Wallace shouted as Reagan was being escorted back outside, "some of these demonstrators think Gorbachev is more a man of peace than you are." Reagan stopped and looked back over his shoulder. He said, "They just have to learn, don't they?" Wallace asked if Reagan was upset by the demonstrations. "I haven't seen any," Reagan said.

The northeast balcony of the Reichstag offered a view of the Spree River and East Berlin, with the television tower at Alexanderplatz looming in the distance. Two East German border guards in a security post on the eastern side of the Wall could be seen filming Reagan with a video camera. A clutch of reporters and news crews joined the dignitaries on the balcony, including Lou Cannon, the *Washington Post*'s White House correspondent. "You could see these heart-rending graffiti and tributes to people crossing the Wall," Cannon said in an interview for this book. "I had read all these things about the Wall, but I had never seen it myself. There were tears in people's eyes. It had an immense emotional impact on people there, including me. And Reagan was affected by it too." Kohl and Diepgen showed Reagan the red crosses painted on the western side of the Wall, each commemorating one of the East Germans killed trying to breach it. Kohl told Reagan that the East Germans watching them in the guard post on the opposite side had listening devices that could pick up their conversation. "They can hear everything we're saying," Kohl said, though Reagan didn't seem concerned. A reporter asked if he thought the Wall would ever come down. "Jericho didn't last forever," Reagan replied.

"This is the only wall that's ever been built to keep people in, not keep people out," Reagan said, a line he had used throughout his career. Duberstein was standing nearby. "He said it with such emotion," Duberstein says, "that I knew he was going to give the speech of a lifetime."

Estimates differ about the number of people in the crowd at the Brandenburg Gate. Reagan recorded in his diary that he addressed "tens & tens of thousands." Kornblum has written that more than forty thousand people attended. The *New York Times* reported that the Berlin police estimated the size to be twenty thousand, "but some observers thought the crowd was smaller than that." Many of the American attendees were packed near the front, within a few feet of the stage. They held their cameras aloft and waved American and German flags. Hooley, the advance man, was disappointed. The crowd seemed smaller and more subdued than he had anticipated. "You had people with babies out there and families with children who had been out there for hours," he said. "It's hard to keep a crowd's enthusiasm under those conditions."

It was nearly 2 P.M. After viewing the Wall from the Reichstag balcony, Reagan got in his limousine for the three-minute ride to the Brandenburg Gate. He was taken to a construction trailer where he was fitted with a bulletproof vest. To the Germans in the trailer, Reagan related a story from his Hollywood days that he often told, about passing time on a movie set with Marlene Dietrich, who taught Reagan how to ask for a match using a perfect German accent (*Haben sie ein Streicholz fur mich, bitte?*). Reagan said that he later used the line on a waiter in a German hotel, who marveled at Reagan's fluency, unaware it was the only German he knew.

Members of the White House staff took up places below the

speaking platform. Tony Dolan later said that as he waited for Reagan to arrive at the site, he saw the sunlight hitting the dome at the top of the Alexanderplatz television tower. He remembered the anecdote Robinson had written into the speech, about how, after building the tower, the East German regime had tried in vain to correct what they thought of as its only flaw: when sunlight hit the dome, it made the sign of the cross. "I looked up and the clouds were parting, and damn if the cross wasn't coming out on top of that tower," Dolan said. "I thought, 'Well that speaks well for what will happen with the speech.'"

On the other side of the Wall, about five hundred people congregated at the intersection of Unter den Linden and Otto Grotewohl Strasse, waiting for the speech to begin. At least half were Stasi agents. According to an internal Security Ministry report, the GDR police kept "negative enemy elements"—such as journalists working for Western publications and members of the opposition—under house arrest during Reagan's speech. Three of Gerd Poppe's colleagues were arrested in the vicinity of the Unter den Linden, on suspicion they were headed there to try to listen to Reagan's speech. As it turns out, there wasn't much to hear. Though Reagan would address "those listening in East Berlin," it's doubtful very many heard it live; the East Germans had pushed the security perimeter so far back from the Brandenburg Gate that Reagan was nearly inaudible. Stasi agents checked the IDs of youths in the crowd and secretly photographed everyone there. A U.S. diplomat strolling among the crowd on Unter den Linden reported that just before 2 P.M., a voice came over a loudspeaker instructing people to disperse, but most stayed put. When police moved in to push people along, one man refused, saying he paid taxes and could stand where he pleased. "Police and public settled down for a very quiet hour," the diplomat reported. "The tops of flags waved by the crowd listening to the President occasionally appeared over the Wall through the arches of the Brandenburg Gate. Otherwise, nothing could be seen or heard." Still, many East Germans remained there, talking quietly and looking at the Wall.

Svetlana Savranskaya could see the movement of figures on the stage through the bulletproof glass. She could tell Reagan was about to begin speaking. At that moment a man in civilian clothes tapped her on the shoulder. He spoke to her in plain Russian. "You are a Soviet citizen," he said. "You need to leave this place immediately." Svetlana was too stunned to speak. He repeated the order. "Leave right now or there will be consequences." The KGB agent followed her as she started walking up the boulevard. When she believed she had shaken him, she moved to the back of the crowd. Again she strained to catch a glimpse of Reagan through the gaps between the columns of the Gate. Then a second man turned to her, showed her a badge and said in Russian, "You are a Soviet citizen. You have no right to be here." This time Svetlana obeyed.

The crowd cheered Reagan for a full minute after he climbed the dais. He acknowledged the cheers with a broad grin and an emphatic thumbs-up. The reception visibly energized him. He took his seat next to Kohl and listened to Diepgen's introductory remarks in German. Kohl spoke next, giving a brief but deeply felt address about the pain to people in both East and West caused by Berlin's division. "It hurts us that Berliners have to celebrate their city's anniversary separated. We have not accepted it in the past and we do not accept it today. We know that a wall, barbed wire and shooting orders are not the answer to the German question." When he was finished, Kohl sat down and prompted Reagan to take the lectern. As Reagan stood, there was a boisterous ovation from the audience, at which point the dignitaries seated on the stage—twenty-four in all—got up to applaud as well. The crowd quieted quickly. Reagan began.

"Twenty-four years ago, President John F. Kennedy visited Berlin," he said. Since then two other presidents had come, and he was there for a second time. His tone was measured, conversational, subdued. Like an ice skater about to execute a difficult jump, he slowed as he neared the first German line: "I come here today because wherever I go, whatever I do, *Ich hab noch einen Koffer in Berlin*" (I always leave a suitcase in Berlin). The line drew laughter and applause. Reagan smiled with relief, evidently pleased with himself. "Behind me stands a wall that encircles the free sectors of this city, part of a vast system of barriers that divides the entire continent of Europe," Reagan went on. His voice grew louder, the cadence more deliberate. Describing the features of this "system of barriers," he crisply punctuated the words "gash," "barbed wire," "concrete," "dog runs," "guard towers." He warmed to his subject. "As long as this gate is closed, as long as this scar of a wall is permitted to stand, it is not the German question alone that remains open"—he looked up from his notes—"but the question of FREEdom for ALL mankind."

That got the crowd going. And yet there were few applause lines as Reagan moved into the speech's historical section on the Marshall Plan, the rebuilding of postwar Europe, and the growth of West Berlin. He elicited only a few polite chuckles when he read Robinson's line about *"Berliner herz, Berliner humor, ja und Berliner schnauze"*—a German phrase sometimes used to describe the city's resilience. Reagan's delivery was smooth, almost effortless, but hardly electrifying. He was more than ten minutes in when he reached the central passage.

"We hear much from Moscow about a new policy of reform and openness." If the Soviets truly wanted to make peace, there was one way to prove it, Reagan said. "General Secretary Gorbachev, if you seek peace, if you seek prosperity for the Soviet Union and Eastern Europe, if you seek liberalization, come here to this gate." He looked up from the podium, his jaw set and teeth clenched, and paused a beat. "Mr. Gorbachev, OPEN this gate," he said. He was practically shouting, as the historian Richard Reeves wrote. Reagan later told Lou Cannon he felt anger in his voice as he spoke those words. The crowd cheered for close to twenty seconds, perhaps thinking Reagan had reached his rhetorical apex. But he had one more line to deliver. He waited, then started in again. "Mr. Gorbachev," he said, but the crowd was drowning him out.

At that moment, Tom Griscom's heart sank. He had listened to Reagan deliver the line about the Wall in the Oval Office, had fought to keep it in the speech, insisted to the secretary of state that its resonance as a sound bite was more important than any diplomatic feathers it might ruffle. Now people might not even hear it. "We missed this one," he said to himself. "We were wrong." But then Reagan paused. He looked down at his notes and waited for the noise to subside. Finally it did.

"Mr. Gorbachev, tear DOWN this Wall!"

Peter Robinson watched the speech at his apartment in Alexandria, Virginia. As he wrote the words of the address, he had often imagined how Reagan would say them. But even he was unprepared for the force of the president's voice when he delivered the climactic line. "With Reagan, you could hear him when you wrote and then he delivered—and it would almost always be better," Robinson says. Watching the speech that morning, Robinson heard for the first time the natural rhythm of the phrase "tear down this Wall." "I don't believe I thought of it this way," Robinson said. "But you have four single syllables there. You can hit them and sound almost like hammer blows. Tear. Down. This. Wall. And that's exactly what he did."

Howard Baker, the White House chief of staff, had initially pushed to remove the "tear down this Wall" line, saying it was unpresidential. But once he heard Reagan deliver it in Berlin, Baker knew instantly he had been wrong to oppose it. "I'd been wrestling with the speech for weeks, but I was stunned at how effective that line sounded. Only Reagan could give it that flair and weight," he said, adding, "I was glad not to be right about this." Richard von Weizsäcker, the West German president, was sitting to the right of the lectern. "He managed to capture in one sentence the essence of the matter," Weizsäcker said years later. "It was the highest form of political expression." And yet at the time few recognized the moment as iconic. Reagan biographer Edmund Morris, who was in Berlin, wrote at the time that the speech was "too staged, the crowd too small and well-primed to make for genuine drama. . . . What a rhetorical opportunity missed." Bredow recalled that the Americans near the stage "went absolutely wild with enthusiasm," but the Germans in the crowd were only politely applauding. "It sounded wonderful," he said. "But most of us thought, 'Ah yes. It will have to wait a long time.'" Reagan's national security adviser, Frank Carlucci, was watching the speech just offstage. "It's a great speech line," he thought to himself. "But it will never happen."

The crowd hollered, clapped, and whistled for fifteen seconds after Reagan delivered the line. The rest of the speech was less memorable, though Reagan continued to show flashes of emotion. He outlined the progress the United States and Moscow had made in arms control talks, but pointed out that it was NATO's deployment of missiles in Western Europe that had convinced the Soviets they had to negotiate. Almost scowling, he said, "I invite those who protest today to mark this fact. Because we remained strong, the Soviets came BACK to the table." That was a crowd-pleaser, and yet some of his most prescient lines were practically ignored. "In this age of information and innovation, the Soviet Union must make a choice," he later said. "It must make fundamental changes, or it will become obsolete." The audience reaction was tepid. It seemed like a throwaway prediction, without any real grounding in reality; only with hindsight can we see that Reagan called it right.

The president spoke for twenty-eight minutes. His tone was almost hushed as he concluded with the story of the television tower at Alexanderplatz, the "secular structure" erected by the communists in place of churches. "Even today when the sun strikes that sphere—that sphere that towers over all Berlin—the light makes the sign of the cross," he said, drawing the most emotional response of the day. When he came to the end, he looked up from his note cards. Though Reagan had earlier brushed aside reporters' questions about the demonstrations against his visit, they had clearly struck a nerve. He departed from the written text, his expression turning from amusement to disdain as he ad-libbed. "I would like to say one thing" to the demonstrators. "I wonder if they have ever asked themselves, that if they should have the kind of government they apparently seek"—he slowed down, making each word sound like a rebuke—"no one would ever be able to do what they're doing again." The audience roared. Reagan waited until the noise subsided, then said, "Thank you and God bless you all." He flashed a thumbs-up to the crowd and shook hands with Kohl. He waved a final time and exited stage left, holding Nancy's hand.

As it happened, the protests meant to coincide with Reagan's speech never took place. The German authorities were so concerned about the possibility of riots that they obtained a court order banning all four of the scheduled outdoor rallies. As of noon, subway service had been suspended out of Kreuzberg, the nerve center of the radical scene. If the anarchists wanted to cause trouble in the center of town, they would have to walk there. A standoff between police and about five hundred protesters on the Kurfürstendamm grew tense that evening, but by then Reagan was gone.

Reviews of the speech were mixed. In West Germany, the daily *Die Welt* called it a "highly political yet casually and brilliantly recited speech." The right-leaning German newspaper *Frankfurter Allgemeine* predicted that Reagan's words "will reach millions of people in GDR and other communist countries" but also concluded, "Gorbachev will not tear down the Wall, and Reagan knows it." The Russian news agency TASS called it "an openly provocative, war-mongering speech." The *New York Times* and the *Washington Post* ran photographs of Reagan in Berlin on their front pages, but buried accounts of the speech inside. All three network newscasts led with reports from Berlin and replayed the challenge to Gorbachev in its entirety. ABC's Sam Donaldson said that "[Reagan's] dramatic words and imagery lifted his own spirits as well as those of this city." NBC's Chris Wallace said the speech was "reminiscent of 1963" but that "U.S.-Soviet relations are far more complicated" than at the time of Kennedy's visit. He reminded American viewers that "polls indicate West Germans view Mr. Gorbachev as more a man of peace than Reagan." On ABC, Henry Kissinger provided commentary on Reagan's performance. The speech was "very effective," Kissinger said. Asked if the Soviets might relax their policies in Berlin, he said, "They might relax them to some extent. But they won't tear down the Wall."

Even to those who witnessed Reagan's speech in person, the Wall seemed immovable. Reagan's challenge to Gorbachev had been great theater, but few imagined that anything would come of it. Jim Kuhn, one of Reagan's longest-serving aides, had watched the speech from a spot close to the platform. He saw the president minutes after he left the stage. Reagan was in a good mood, still basking in the ovation from the crowd. Kuhn felt more ambivalent. As he congratulated Reagan on his performance, Kuhn thought to himself, This man will never live to see the day when that Wall comes down.

After the speech, Reagan headed back to Tempelhof Airport. Members of the U.S. military and their families had been invited there for the birthday party in honor of Berlin's 750th anniversary. The crowd was raucous. They ate hamburgers and hot dogs and drank Budweiser. Burt introduced Reagan. "I could just tell he was really happy," Burt said. Reagan opened his remarks with jokes. "It's not often I get to go to a birthday party for something that's older than I am," he said, breaking up the room. His speech paid tribute to the citizens of the city and the U.S. servicemen based there. "Our troops will remain here as long as they are wanted and needed by Berliners." In the middle of his remarks, there was a sound eerily like a gunshot. It was a balloon popping. "Missed me," Reagan said, without skipping a beat.

Before leaving Berlin, Reagan placed a three-minute phone call to Margaret Thatcher. She had just won reelection and Reagan told her he was pleased with the result. Thatcher said the margin of victory had exceeded her expectations. She would remain in office another three or four years, she told Reagan. Then she asked, "Are you having a good day in Berlin?" Reagan told her that he had spoken before the Brandenburg Gate and called for the Wall to come down. He thought that line had been especially well received. Thatcher replied that she had heard that the crowd roared in approval. She said she hoped to come to the U.S. in the summer "for a long talk" with Reagan before he went on vacation. "Love to Nancy," she said.

The president left Berlin at 4:47 in the afternoon. The American delegation flew to Bonn, where Reagan and Kohl met for forty-five minutes, in a VIP lounge at the Cologne-Bonn airport. William Bodde, the Undersecretary of State for European affairs, recalls that the men didn't discuss the substance of Reagan's speech at the Brandenburg Gate. Kohl brought up the pope, who was visiting Poland. "You know, Ronnie," Kohl said, "he had a million people come to see him." Reagan smiled. "If I could draw those crowds, I would have stayed in Hollywood." They went outside for the departure ceremony. "This was a memorable day," Kohl told Reagan. "You have renewed the American commitment to Berlin and for Germany as a whole in a moving speech."

It was just after seven in the evening. Reagan said goodbye to Kohl on the red carpet, then charged up the stairs and boarded Air Force One. He drifted into the main cabin and made small talk with members of his staff, then retired to the State Room with Nancy. Reagan pulled out his diary to record the day's events. "Met several elderly ladies who had been part of the female force that cleaned bricks and rubble & played a role in Berlin's rebuilding," he wrote. "Then it was on to the Brandenburg Gate where I addressed tens &

tens of thousands of people—stretching as far as I could see. I got a tremendous reception—interrupted 28 times by cheers."

Air Force One arrived at Andrews Air Force Base a little after 10 P.M. Reagan couldn't resist recording that "we traveled in bright sunshine" for nearly the entire flight. "It didn't get dark until a little less than an hour out and yet it was after 3 A.M. back where we left." It had been nearly twenty-four hours since his day began in Venice. Marine One whisked the Reagans to the South Lawn. They walked into the White House. "Well," Reagan wrote, "home at last."

9. MIKHAIL AND RON

A few days after returning to Washington, Tony Dolan sent a memo to the president. "We're grateful for your kind words on the Berlin draft," Dolan wrote to Reagan, adding that he had passed on the compliments to Peter Robinson. "In view of all you told us about what you wanted in Berlin—including the outline and the killer lines you gave us—it was particularly generous of you." Dolan was being generous too. As far as Robinson can recollect, Reagan had made only one comment after the original draft of the speech was submitted to him: he liked the line about tearing down the Berlin Wall. If the president gave Dolan anything resembling an "outline" for the speech, Dolan never shared it with Robinson. There's no documentary evidence that Reagan's involvement in drafting the speech was near as extensive as Dolan's memo suggests. Perhaps Dolan was simply following the cardinal rule of the speechwriters: let the president take full credit for his speeches. "You have always been the author of your own success," Dolan wrote to Reagan, laying it on thick. "That will be the unquestioned judgment of history, too." The speechwriters liked to tell people that "most of what we do over here is plagiarize your old speeches or take good notes about where you want to go in a speech."

At 8 P.M. that evening, Reagan addressed the nation from the

Oval Office. He talked about his discussions with other leaders at the Venice summit, the budget making its way through Congress, and the progress of arms reduction talks with Moscow. He announced that the United States had agreed to the outlines of a deal to remove all intermediate-range nuclear missiles in Europe and eliminate short-range nuclear missiles worldwide. Berlin was still fresh in his mind. "I must make a personal note about something we saw on the last day of our journey," he said. "No American who sees firsthand the concrete and mortar, the guard posts and machine gun towers, the dog runs and the barbed wire can ever take for granted his or her freedom." The desire to spread freedom is why "I urged the Soviet leader, Mr. Gorbachev, to send a new signal of openness to the world by tearing down that Wall."

Interviewed years later, Gorbachev downplayed the speech's impact on his thinking, complimenting Reagan as "a good actor" but dismissing any suggestion that it had influenced his policies.* Gorbachev was pushing changes on his own. He had told the leaders in the Warsaw Pact countries they needed to open up their political system, or face oblivion. He planned to reduce the Red Army's presence in Eastern Europe. As the historian Melvyn Leffler wrote in his book *For the Soul of Mankind*, Gorbachev had come to believe that "if the Kremlin demonstrated that shared values united, rather than divided mankind, it could relax tensions and nurture more peaceful relationships."

Did that include taking down the Berlin Wall? Doing so was not a pressing priority for Gorbachev. But he remained more open to the idea of German reunification than many of his comrades. And he sensed that the repressiveness and intransigence of the East

---

* The speech seemed to make a deeper impression on East German leader Erich Honecker, who was irritated that Reagan called on Gorbachev, not Honecker, to tear down the Wall. Honecker was said to believe that Reagan's speech was part of a secret deal between Washington and the Kremlin to let the GDR collapse. See Mann, *The Rebellion of Ronald Reagan*, pp. 209–211.

German communists would someday backfire against them. In the days after Reagan's speech, reports emerged suggesting that Moscow had ordered the East Germans to remove some checkpoints at the Wall and allow more East Berliners to visit West Berlin. Around that time, Peter Rodman, the NSC official who had pushed for revisions in the Brandenburg Gate speech, sat down next to Peter Robinson in the White House mess. "Well, Peter, it looks like *our* speech was a big success," he said. Robinson held his tongue. Rodman told him that U.S. intelligence services had intercepted cable traffic between Moscow and Berlin. The Kremlin was pressuring the Honecker government to loosen restrictions at the Berlin Wall, Rodman said, adding that each new generation of Soviet leaders needed to be reminded what a public relations disaster the Wall was. Robinson disagreed. The Wall wasn't a PR disaster. It was an affront to humanity.

In West Germany, U.S. officials fielded predictable complaints about Reagan's rhetoric from their Soviet counterparts. But the president may have tapped into a sense among some Russians that the ground was shifting beneath them. In early July, U.S. ambassador Burt had lunch in Berlin with Vyacheslav Kochemassov, the USSR's ambassador to East Germany. Kochemassov expressed "regret and sadness" at the tone and content of Reagan's speech. The Soviets had studied it closely but "found no basis on which to proceed." Burt told Kochemassov that "the president is a man with strong beliefs, none of which are stronger than his belief that the tragic division of Berlin should be ended. The speech was not propaganda but spoken from the heart." As Burt went on, Kochemassov relaxed. He agreed that the Germans would not accept the division of their country forever. "Change is inevitable," Burt told his counterpart. "And your country would be making a mistake of historic proportions to resist it." The Russian smiled in agreement.

Reagan himself was not given to reflection. He could regale audiences with stories from his Hollywood days, but almost never reminisced about earlier moments in his presidency. He treated each day as if it were his first in office, reflected in the daily diary entries he made to mark even the quotidian events. He did not look back. The memo Dolan sent to the president on June 15 indicates that Reagan complimented the speechwriters on the Berlin speech shortly after he gave it. There's no evidence he spent much more time dwelling on that day in Berlin. But others did.* Not long after Reagan returned from Europe, Andrew Littlefair, a member of the president's Advance Office, was in a holding room with the president before one of his speeches. Jim Kuhn, one of Reagan's aides, mentioned to Reagan that Littlefair had helped in the arrangements for the speech at the Berlin Wall. "I don't know why Gorbachev doesn't do it," Reagan said. "If he took down that Wall, he'd win the Nobel Prize."

Reagan continued to push the idea. His rhetoric toward the Soviets still alternated between standard denunciations of the communist system and more conciliatory acknowledgments of Gorbachev's efforts to reform it. Even as conservatives stepped up their attacks on him for negotiating an arms reduction treaty with the Russians, Reagan refused to alter his course. He was starting to see Gorbachev as a transformative figure, the kind of leader who might be willing not just to halt the arms race but also open up the East-

---

* In late June Carlucci forwarded Reagan a letter from Mstislav Rostropovich, the great Russian émigré cellist, who along with his wife, Galina, was scheduled to meet the president in person. "I am delighted that today, one of the happiest days of my life, I will have the opportunity to thank you personally for the Berlin speech," Rostropovich wrote, "which excited Galina and me to the depths of our souls." Rostropovich asked for Reagan's help in convincing the Soviets to allow a religious dissident named Igor Ogurtsov, who had served twenty years in the Soviet gulag, to leave the country. Reagan wrote back to Frank Carlucci by hand, "What if I asked Gorbachev personally—my request that he let Ogurtsov leave Russia?" (The Soviets eventually did exile Ogurtsov to East Germany.)

ern Bloc—even though some of his own intelligence officials were making the exact opposite case.

A little more than a month after the Berlin speech, Reagan returned to the subject of the Wall in a speech in Washington. "Last month when I was in Berlin, I called on Soviet leader Gorbachev to prove to the world that his glasnost campaign is more than words," he said. "I challenged him to tear down the Berlin Wall and to open the Brandenburg Gate. I renew that challenge today," adding that Gorbachev should remove the yoke of Soviet "domination" over the Baltic states and Eastern Europe. He inserted by hand the sentence, "There are indications of change coming from the Soviet Union, and those are welcomed."

Two weeks later, Reagan devoted his radio address to marking "a dark anniversary"—the twenty-sixth year since the construction of the Berlin Wall. "Glasnost is a Russian word that we're told means 'openness.' But does it mean genuine openness to speak, to write, to travel, even to buy or sell? Or is it more of a publicity show?" The way for the Soviets to demonstrate that openness "is to tear down that Wall." He called on Moscow to permit free elections in Eastern Europe but refrained from mentioning Gorbachev by name. He was trying hard not to embarrass him. "Let us resolve to do all we can do to hasten the day when the Wall is down," Reagan said, "and Berlin has become a symbol not of confrontation, but of cooperation among the peoples of Europe and the entire world."

While their negotiators in Geneva hammered out the details of a treaty on eliminating short- and medium-range missiles, Reagan and Gorbachev renewed their correspondence, exchanging formal messages about the Iran-Iraq War. In September, Soviet foreign minister Shevardnadze came to Washington to meet Shultz and Reagan and finalize the terms of the INF treaty. He carried with him a personal greeting from the Gorbachevs to the Reagans and a letter to the U.S. president. "I think you and I were right" Gorbachev's letter began, pointing out that both he and Reagan had concluded after Reykjavik that significant arms reductions were possible. Now the two countries stood "on the threshold" of a treaty that would get rid of some nuclear weapons and show the world "that genuine security can only be achieved through real disarmament." The question is whether the two leaders would follow through and whether a final agreement would be signed or set aside. "It is time you and I took a firm stand," Gorbachev wrote.

Reagan wanted Gorbachev to come to Washington to sign the treaty. He wrote him that he looked forward "to the day when you and I can come together to sign even more historic agreements in our common search for peace." His meeting with Shevardnadze had been a step in that direction. "They were good meetings and free of the hostility we used to see," he noted in his diary. He concluded his letter to Gorbachev: "Nancy and I wish to take this opportunity to convey to you and Mrs. Gorbachev our personal best wishes and our hope that the coming months will see further steps toward our common goals."

A month later, Shultz met with Gorbachev in Moscow. He expected to leave with a commitment from the Soviet leader to come to Washington for a summit with Reagan. But Gorbachev told Shultz he would come to Washington only if the two sides also agreed to eliminate long-range strategic weapons and kill the Star Wars defense shield. Shultz called Reagan to tell him that while a deal on the treaty was likely, Gorbachev's demands may have scuttled the hoped-for summit. "I think we should pass," he said. "We shouldn't push for this." Reagan was furious at Gorbachev—"I think he feels [Congress] has me on ropes & I need a summit"—and said he would refuse to compromise on missile defense. Reports of the abortive summit deal coincided with a stock market crash and the defeat of Robert Bork's nomination to the Supreme Court, leading some in the media to call it the worst week in the history of the Reagan administration, "apparently forgetting Iran-Contra," Shultz later wrote.

Then Gorbachev backed away. He had Shevardnadze return to Washington with a letter to Reagan proposing the "total elimination of the entire class of missiles with ranges between 500 and 5,500 kilometers and of all warheads for those missiles." He skirted the issue of Star Wars. He proposed coming for a summit in Washington "in the first ten days of December." Shultz told Reagan the U.S. should agree to the deal. Reagan was impressed by Gorbachev's letter. "It is statesmanlike & indicated a real desire for us to work out any differences." After Reagan met with Shevardnadze, the two sides agreed to a summit beginning December 7. Reagan and Gorbachev would sign the first U.S.-Soviet treaty ever to get *rid* of nuclear weapons, rather than just limit them. If all went as planned, Reagan would go to Moscow the following spring to sign a deal reducing long-range missiles as well.

Possibility was in the air. "I felt that a profound, historic shift was underway. The Soviet Union was willingly or unwillingly, consciously or not, turning a corner," Shultz said. "They were not just resting for round two of the cold war." Neither was the president.

Though there were few tangible signs that Reagan's speech in Berlin had actually produced movement toward bringing down the Wall, the speechwriters searched for ways for Reagan to keep talking about it. In early November, Dana Rohrabacher drafted remarks that Reagan would deliver to satellite television viewers in Western Europe. The draft read, "In a few weeks General Secretary Gorbachev will visit me here in Washington. During our discussions I will offer to meet him in Berlin on any day of his choosing so that together we can take down the first bricks of that Wall . . . Mr. Gorbachev, let us lead the way. Let us take down that Wall." When the draft was returned to Rohrabacher with comments from the NSC, the entire section had been circled and crossed out, the word NO written in the margin. Rohrabacher rewrote the passage: "Wouldn't it be a wonderful sight for the world to see, if someday General Secretary Gorbachev and I could meet in Berlin and together take down the first bricks of that Wall—and we could continue taking down the walls until the distrust between our peoples and the scars of the past are forgotten?" Again the NSC objected, sending back an edited version of the speech with the Berlin section highlighted. "Looks like we share the responsibility. Better to drop." But this time the language stayed.

Gorbachev arrived in Washington a little more than a month later, on December 7, 1987. It was the first superpower summit held in the United States in fourteen years. Gorbachev and his wife, Raisa, were met at Andrews Air Force Base by Secretary Shultz. "The visit has begun, so let's hope," Gorbachev said on the tarmac. "We are ready," Shultz said. "We're ready too," Gorbachev responded. A fifty-vehicle motorcade took the Soviet leader into downtown Washington, reaching the barricaded Soviet embassy on 16th Street at 5:19 P.M.

The city was gripped by Gorbymania. "Wherever he went," wrote Lou Cannon, "crowds lined the street to applaud him." Gorbachev had never been to America. He wanted to see other parts of the country, as Reagan had encouraged, but the Soviet security services believed it was too risky for him to venture beyond Washington. After arriving at the embassy, Gorbachev had tea with Shultz and addressed a select group of American celebrities, including Henry Kissinger, Paul Newman, and Yoko Ono. "I feel that something serious is afoot, something that embraces broad sections of the people, an awareness that we cannot go on as we are."

Gorbachev met Reagan at the White House on December 8. "This is the big day," Reagan wrote in his diary. The president greeted Gorbachev on the South Lawn at 10 A.M., then took him inside for a meeting in the Oval Office, with only interpreters present. Reagan criticized the Soviets' human rights record, only to hear Gorbachev claim that Russian citizens had more rights than

Americans. After lunch the two leaders went to the East Room to sign the INF Treaty, on a table once used by Abraham Lincoln. At the signing ceremony, Reagan stressed that this was the first U.S.-Soviet treaty to require both sides to destroy nuclear weapons. "We have listened to an old Russian maxim," Reagan said, before repeating his favorite (and maybe only) Russian phrase: "*Doveryay, no proveryay*—trust, but verify." Gorbachev rolled his eyes. "You repeat that at every meeting," he said. "I like it," Reagan replied. (The historian Sean Wilentz later commented, "The superpowers' antagonism had turned into vaudeville repartee.")

Despite their obvious ease together, the two leaders were very different men. Reagan's relentless jocularity and inattention to details mystified the intensely focused Gorbachev. After the signing ceremony, the two were joined by their staffs for plenary sessions. While Gorbachev gave a detailed briefing on his program of perestroika, Reagan told an old joke about a man heading to Russia on a trip. On the way to the airport, the man asked his young taxi driver what he wanted to be in life. The young man replied that he hadn't decided. When the man arrived in Moscow, he put the same question to his Russian taxi driver, also a young man finishing his education. "They haven't told me yet," the Russian replied.

Gorbachev wasn't amused. He was so annoyed by what he perceived as Reagan's lack of seriousness that he threatened to end the conversation, until Shultz intervened. Afterward, Shultz and Baker took Reagan aside. The president knew he had bungled the meeting. "I guess I shouldn't have told that joke," he said. The next day, Reagan went outside at 10:30 A.M. "to meet Gorby (I should say Mikhail)," as he wrote in his diary. At their meeting that morning, Reagan was in better form, as the two discussed the possibility of signing a strategic arms agreement when Reagan came to Moscow in the spring. He pressed Gorbachev to set a date for pulling out from Afghanistan, telling him that the U.S. would do its part to help if the Soviet Union withdrew.

Then Reagan brought up Berlin. The city could be the site of positive developments, he said. The two sides could take small steps to ease the division of the city, which would be a sign of their shared commitment to ending the division of Europe into Western and communist blocs. He urged Gorbachev to act boldly. You should take down the Wall, Reagan told him. You can do it.

Gorbachev did not respond directly. He was an intensely proud, self-confident man who did not like to be told what to do. Even Reagan later admitted that "things got a little heated." Gorbachev cut Reagan off during one of his lectures. "Mr. President, you are not a prosecutor and I am not on trial here. Like you, I represent a great country and therefore expect our dialogue to be conducted on a basis of reciprocity and equality. Otherwise there simply will be no dialogue." And yet by now Gorbachev knew Reagan well enough. The American president could be maddeningly vague, stubborn, and facile, all at the same time. But he was utterly genuine in his desire to end the enmity that had separated the superpowers for half a century. He was not out to humiliate Gorbachev. "Reagan never claimed victory," says Jack Matlock, the U.S. ambassador to Moscow at the time. "He wanted to get into a real negotiation and for that you had to stop treating it like a sports contest, with scores and a winner and a loser."

On Gorbachev's last day at the White House, Reagan gave him a baseball to sign. Joe DiMaggio had been a guest at the previous night's dinner in honor of the Gorbachevs and had asked Reagan to get the Soviet leader's autograph. Gorbachev suggested Reagan visit Moscow in May, before the weather got too hot. Reagan said that, perhaps before he left office, Gorbachev could come back to the U.S. to see the rest of the country. "You haven't seen America until you've seen California," Reagan said.

When the two delegations met for a final working lunch in the White House's family dining room, Gorbachev said that while he was known all over the world, he still remained a man from the provinces.

There was more common sense among ordinary people there than was to be found in the Kremlin. Reagan told him that he agreed with that sentiment "more completely" than anything else Gorbachev had said in the previous three days. "I often wonder what would happen if we closed the doors of our offices and quietly slipped away," Reagan said. "How long would it be before people missed us?"

At the end of the lunch, Reagan told Gorbachev they had a right to feel good about the summit. He reminded him of their first meeting in Geneva, when he had said that between them "they could initiate another world war or make sure that there would not be another world war." Gorbachev remembered the conversation. "We don't want to have to defend ourselves one day by saying we did nothing," he said, "when we could have acted." That night, Reagan went before the nation to report on the summit. His tone was typically upbeat. One section of the draft from the speechwriters had read, "we are saying that the postwar policy of containment is no longer enough, that the goal of American foreign policy is both world peace and world freedom, that as a people we hope and will work for a day when all of God's children will enjoy the human dignity that their creator intended." After that sentence, Reagan had inserted by hand, "I believe we gained some ground with regard to that cause in these last few weeks." At the bottom of the draft, Reagan had scribbled another note: "Add an optimistic (not pie in the sky) but a legitimate sum-up of progress made." The speechwriters complied. "Mr. Gorbachev and I have agreed to meet in several months in Moscow to continue what we have achieved in these past three days," Reagan said that night. "I believe there is reason for both hope and optimism."

The trip to Washington changed Gorbachev. He had been stunned at the reception he received among ordinary Americans, the crowds that mobbed him on Connecticut Avenue when he got out of his limousine, the letters and greetings that flooded the Soviet embassy while he was there. He came away convinced that Americans, as Reagan had assured him years before, had no interest in war with the Soviet Union. "The friendly atmosphere, even enthusiasm . . . with which straight-laced Washington met us, was a sign of the changes that have begun to transpire in the West," he told his comrades upon returning to Moscow. "The enemy image had begun to erode, and the myth of the 'Soviet military threat' was undermined. It was very special for us."

The knowledge that Americans no longer viewed the USSR as a mortal enemy was liberating. Gorbachev began to speak more openly about the common humanity between capitalist and socialist societies. And he told others in the Kremlin that the Soviet Union needed to take steps to ease the "perception of threat" that the country posed to the West. In Gorbachev's mind, that meant continued liberalization of the Soviet political system, further cuts in military spending, an easing of Moscow's grip on Eastern Europe, and withdrawal of Soviet troops from Afghanistan.

Reagan's agenda was less ambitious. The last year of his presidency would be largely overshadowed by the campaign to succeed him. Stories of his mental lapses and tendency to doze off during staff meetings were by now legend. And yet thanks to his summitry with Gorbachev, Reagan's popularity had recovered from the depths to which it had slid after Iran-contra. That helped the White House fend off attempts by the Republican Party's conservative wing to kill the denuclearization agreement Reagan signed with Gorbachev. Sixty percent of Americans told pollsters they thought the U.S. Senate should ratify the agreement solely because Reagan said it was a good deal. The president privately assured skeptical conservatives that he wasn't compromising national security—"Gorby knows what our response to cheating would be—it's spelled Pershing," he wrote to William F. Buckley—but he remained steadfast in his desire to see an end to the arms race.

After reading an essay in *Newsweek* by Henry Kissinger warning that the INF treaty could tilt the balance of power in Europe toward the Soviets, Reagan wrote to a supporter, "I respect Henry Kissinger and consider him a good friend but in this instance do not believe he is fully informed. A nuclear war cannot be won and must never be fought." It was a line that he repeated often in the latter stages of his presidency. His analysis was simple enough to be understood by schoolchildren. "In such a war between the two great powers," he wrote, "one has to ask if ever we launched those weapons at each other where would the survivors live?"

With much of the Republican establishment's attention trained on the presidential primaries, the White House focused on winning ratification for the INF treaty and planning Reagan's trip to Moscow. That spring, Josh Gilder accompanied the advance team to Russia. Gilder had worked in the speechwriting office for three years. He came from an unconventional background—he was raised in a family of socialists—but possessed the zeal of a True Believer. The speeches he wrote for Reagan often talked about how the coming revolution in information technology would render obsolete state-run command economies like the Soviet Union's. For the summit, Gilder was assigned to write the speech the president would give to students at Moscow State University.

When the advance team arrived in Moscow, a Russian official took the Americans to the auditorium selected for the event. "It was a huge building, very forbidding when you entered it, but inside there was this really quite beautiful marble auditorium," Gilder says. "And behind the stage was a mosaic of the October Revolution with all these red flags, right? And standing right there on the stage was this massive bust of Lenin." Gilder turned to his hosts. "The bust has to go," he said. "And you've got to cover up the mural." The Russian official pleaded with him, but Gilder insisted. The Russian was crestfallen. But then Gilder had an inspiration. "You know what it's like when you're writing, you get the hook? I got the opening."

Reagan would invoke the symbols of the Bolshevik Revolution to tell the students about a new revolution—a tidal wave of free markets, technology, and democracy sweeping the world. Gilder went back to his host. "You know what? Keep the bust," he said.

On May 27, the Senate ratified the INF Treaty by a vote of 93–5. Two days later, the Reagans arrived in Moscow. In an interview with Soviet television journalists, the president had been asked if he considered Gorbachev "a friend." Reagan replied, "Well, I can't help but say yes to that, because the difference that I've found between him and other leaders is that yes, we can debate and disagree. . . . But there is never a sense of personal animus." Little of policy substance was achieved at the Moscow summit. The two sides had not settled on the terms of an agreement to reduce long-range nuclear weapons, and they remained at loggerheads over missile defense. But that mattered little to the two leaders, who knew this might be their last meeting as heads of state. As in Washington, Reagan and Gorbachev traded bons mots and talked about the possibilities for world peace. Gorbachev told Reagan it was a shame that just when the Kremlin had established good relations with the administration, an election for a new president came along. Reagan responded by saying that, even if wasn't proper protocol, between the two of them they were just two friends, Mikhail and Ron.

The White House had devised a meticulous script for the summit, bracketing the Reagan-Gorbachev meetings with visits to monasteries and churches, conversations with dissidents and photo ops at Moscow's historic landmarks. The only hitch came on the Reagans' first day, when the first couple decided to take a stroll along the Arbat, one of Moscow's famous pedestrian streets. When word spread that Reagan was there, an excited mob of Russians converged on the street, hoping to catch a glimpse of him. KGB agents responded impulsively, beating and shoving people out of the way in plain view of the Reagans. "It's still a police state," Reagan muttered under his breath.

The rest of the trip surpassed the expectations of all but the most hardened Cold Warriors. In those four days in Moscow, Reagan and Gorbachev buried once and for all the specter of superpower conflict. "The Soviet people have a high regard for you, Mr. President, and for the American people," Gorbachev said. In one of the early meetings, Gorbachev presented Reagan with a statement to be released jointly at the end of the summit. "The two leaders believe that no problem in dispute can be resolved, nor should it be resolved, by military means. They regard peaceful coexistence as a universal principle of international relations," the statement read. "I like it," Reagan said.

At the end of their one-hour session at the Kremlin on the morning of May 31, Gorbachev suggested they go for a walk. This too had been scripted by White House planners, the two friends strolling through Red Square in the glow of early summer. Tourists rushed up to take pictures and chat with Reagan. ABC's Sam Donaldson called out, "Do you still think you're in an Evil Empire, Mr. President?" Without hesitation, Reagan said, "No. That was another time, another era." Standing next to Reagan, Gorbachev was deeply moved. To him, Reagan's statement was the culmination of three years of dialogue between the two most powerful men in the world, in which both had sought to show the other he had nothing to fear. "It meant that he had finally convinced himself that he had been right to believe, back in Reykjavik, that you could do business with the changing Soviet Union—the hopeful business of preventing a nuclear war," Gorbachev wrote years later. "He could congratulate himself on having made the right choice."

Later that day, Reagan addressed the students of Moscow State University. Gilder's draft had not incited an interagency fight like the one over the Brandenburg Gate speech, but significant differences existed between the White House and the State Department. A May 18 memo from State to Colin Powell said "there is a risk of losing the Soviet audience if the tone becomes too preachy. We recommend that the paragraph on Page 9 be dropped." The draft referred to Gorbachev's reforms as "this Moscow spring." State was in favor of dropping that too: "The reforms do not yet add up to changes as far reaching as the Prague Spring of 1968, which the phrase inevitably conjures up." And Gilder had referred to the two leaders' ongoing discussion about taking down the Berlin Wall. "We see no advantage to mentioning the Berlin Wall publicly in Moscow," the memo said. In the end, State lost the battles.

Reagan delivered his speech to an audience of faculty and students, hand-selected and carefully screened by the KGB. It was stiflingly hot in the auditorium, which was not air-conditioned. Reagan's speech ranged widely, with considerations of the power contained in a single computer chip, the role of religion in free societies, and the lessons of the movie *Butch Cassidy and the Sundance Kid*. Freedom, he said, "is the right to question and change the established way of doing things. It is the continuing revolution of the marketplace. . . . It is the right to put forth an idea, scoffed at by the experts, and watch it catch fire among the people. It is the right to dream—to follow your dream or stick to your conscience, even if you're the only one in a sea of doubters." He closed with one of the greatest perorations of his presidency:

"Your generation is living in one of the most exciting, hopeful times in Soviet history. It is a time when the first breath of freedom stirs the air and the heart beats to the accelerated rhythm of hope, when the accumulated spiritual energies of a long silence yearn to break free. We do not know what the conclusion will be of this journey, but we're hopeful that the promise of reform will be fulfilled. In this Moscow spring, this May 1988, we may be allowed that hope: that freedom, like the fresh green sapling planted over Tolstoy's grave, will blossom forth at last in the rich fertile soil of your people and culture. We may be allowed to hope that the marvelous sound of a new openness will keep rising through, ringing through, leading to a new world of reconciliation, friendship, and peace."

The students gave him a standing ovation. Among them was a pregnant 22-year-old woman wearing a bright pink sundress. One year earlier, Svetlana Savranskaya had tried to catch a glimpse of Reagan through the barricades in front of the Brandenburg Gate. On that afternoon, the KGB had chased her away. This time she was one of the Moscow State students chosen to sit in the front row for Reagan's speech. The Russian security officials had warned the students about the Secret Service. "They said, 'If you move, they will shoot you,'" Svetlana remembers. "'Don't make any movements with your body. If you get up, you will be shot.'" In Berlin Reagan was only a distant dot in the landscape; on this day, he was just a few feet away. After the speech, she shook hands with the president. "He spoke to the crowd as if he was speaking to me the whole time," she said. "Here was this American president who seemed so normal. He seemed so warm. He smiled. That speech to me was a revelation. I had a negative image of him, but after that I saw him from a different point of view." As Reagan left the auditorium, an American reporter asked Svetlana what she thought of his speech. She said that what struck her most was the idea that an American president could be a normal human being.

The summit ended with the usual rounds of dinners and toasts. Reagan struggled to stay awake through a performance of the Bolshoi Ballet and one of Gorbachev's speeches. At their last meeting together, he told Gorbachev that he could not sign the statement about "peaceful coexistence" he had agreed to earlier. Reagan's advisers said the phrase was too détentist, too close to the language of accommodation that was anathema to right-wingers. At first Gorbachev couldn't hide his annoyance. "Why are you against it?" he asked, thrusting the paper at Reagan. He turned to Shultz and Carlucci. "What about you, George? Frank? Why not this language?" Gorbachev suggested the Americans discuss the matter again privately. After a few minutes, Reagan walked back toward Gorbachev. "We can't do it," he said. Gorbachev realized that the old negotiator wasn't going to make a deal this time. He smiled and put his arm around Reagan. "Mr. President, we had a great time," he said, and led Reagan out of the room.

"Keep him involved. No coasting," Colin Powell scribbled on a sheet of legal paper at a meeting of the president's advisers in Santa Barbara to plan for Reagan's final six months. Dick Wirthlin, the president's pollster, told the group that Reagan's approval rating was 60 percent, and that 61 percent of Americans approved of his handling of foreign policy, up from 46 percent a year earlier. Powell recorded the themes the White House would promote for the rest of the term: "More change in the right direction." "Peace. Preparing for peace."

In many respects, though, the Moscow summit represented the capstone of Reagan's tenure. He had little left to accomplish. His days were still full of meetings and ceremonial events, but his diary entries show few substantive considerations of policy. At the Republican National Convention, he exhorted Vice President George H. W. Bush to "win one for the Gipper," in a speech rich in sentiment and Reaganesque optimism. "Don't expect me to be happy to hear all this talk about the twilight of my life. Twilight? Twilight? Not in America. Here, it's a sunrise every day. Fresh new opportunities. Dreams to build." For most of the fall campaign, Reagan remained an interested observer, speaking at party fund-raisers and tracking the polls from the White House. In the final week of the campaign, Bush's campaign strategists watched with alarm as the Democratic candidate, Michael Dukakis, pulled even in California. The state's fifty-five electoral votes were suddenly at risk. At the urging of James Baker and Lee Atwater, who ran the Bush campaign, Reagan flew to the state the day before the election. He appeared with the vice president at rallies in Long Beach and San Diego, two GOP strongholds. Bush won California by 3 percentage points—the last

Republican candidate to do so—and took 426 electoral votes, to 111 for Dukakis. When Reagan walked out to the Rose Garden the next morning, his staff cheered. "A very touching moment for me," Reagan wrote in his diary.

Reagan and Gorbachev continued to exchange letters, some formal missives drafted by their staffs covering matters of state, others strikingly personal. "Raisa Maksimovna and I have warm recollections of the hours that we spent in an open and spontaneous give-and-take with Mrs. Reagan and yourself," Gorbachev wrote shortly after the Moscow summit. "We are sending you a photo album." A few months later, Gorbachev gave Shevardnadze another letter to deliver to Reagan in person. The two men had agreed to sustain the spirit of cooperation established in Moscow, "which is a source of great hope for our two peoples." Their four summits "have laid groundwork for our dialogue and raised it a qualitatively new level. And, as we know, from high ground it is easier to see the path we have covered, the problems of the day, and the prospects that emerge." Their partnership was coming to an end, Gorbachev said, but they had set their nations on a path from which they could not turn back. "Our relationship is a dynamic stream and you and I are working together to widen it. The stream cannot be slowed down, it can only be blocked or diverted. But that would not be in our interest."

Despite Reagan's efforts to sell him on the virtues of laissez-faire capitalism, Gorbachev still believed he could save the socialist experiment in the Soviet Union. But that meant abandoning the goal of exporting it abroad. He announced that Soviet troops would depart Afghanistan by early 1989, though he suspected correctly that the United States would continue to aid the fundamentalist mujahedin battling the communist-led government in Kabul. He began pulling Red Army divisions out of Eastern Europe. If the leaders of the Warsaw Pact countries lost the support of their people, the Soviets would not intervene to save them.

In early November, Shultz's deputy, John Whitehead, took a trip to East Berlin to meet with Erich Honecker. The contrasts between East and West were as stark as they had been on Whitehead's last visit to the city, seventeen years earlier. Asked years later what he made of the seventy-six-year-old Honecker, Whitehead said, "silver hair, dogmatic, never smiled. It was hard to have a normal conversation with him." He urged Honecker to tear down the Berlin Wall. If there was one thing that still stood between better relations between East and West, it was the Wall. "The substance of it is where Moscow wants to be. So why don't you just be realistic and take it down and let people go back and forth?" Whitehead asked. He knew the answer. Giving East Germans the freedom to go to the West would lead to the collapse of the GDR. Two months later, Honecker said, "The Wall will still be standing in 50 or 100 years."

On December 7, Reagan and Gorbachev met for the last time as the leaders of the world's two superpowers. Gorbachev had come to New York to meet with Reagan and President-elect Bush and address the General Assembly of the United Nations, where he would call for an end to ideological struggle and announce that the Soviet military would be reduced by half a million men. The three men met on a cold, windswept day on Governors Island, the Statue of Liberty serving as a backdrop. Gorbachev asked Reagan what he should see in New York. "California," Reagan said. "I thought you'd say that," Gorbachev replied. Reagan gave Gorbachev a picture taken of the two of them walking in the woods in Geneva, inscribed with the words, "We have walked a long way together to clear a path for peace." It was signed, Ronald Reagan, Geneva 1985–New York 1988.

The relationship between Ronald Reagan and Mikhail Gorbachev ranks among the most remarkable forged by any two world leaders in modern history. Drawn from different worlds, separated by language and culture, fiercely committed to radically divergent ideologies, they nonetheless managed to find "each in his own way . . . a path out of the Minotaur's lair," as author Richard Rhodes wrote in his book *Arsenals of Folly*. The gravity of the nuclear age had led some of their predecessors to develop deep feelings for each other; Khrushchev was said to have privately wept after hearing of Kennedy's death. But only Reagan and Gorbachev allowed themselves to build enough trust in each other to gamble on change. "Reagan did try to understand where the other guy was coming from, how far you could push, how you could find some common interests," said Jack Matlock. "And that's really the bottom line of what he and Gorbachev were able to do. They were able to find genuine common interests, which required basic changes in Soviet policy. With Gorbachev, Reagan had a partner who was able to understand this. There was probably no other Soviet leader at that time who could have done that."

Neither man claimed credit for himself. Both recognized the enormous moral and political risks the other had taken for the sake of diplomacy and friendship. "In my view, the 40th President of the United States will go down in history for his rare perception," Gorbachev wrote in his memoirs. A decade after both had left office, Gorbachev attended a dinner in Cambridge, England. One of the guests, a British academic, referred to Reagan as a light-weight. "You are wrong," Gorbachev said. "President Reagan was a man of real insight, sound political judgment and courage." And though many of Reagan's acolytes liked to boast that the United States "won" the Cold War, Reagan never did. "Mr. Gorbachev deserves most of the credit," he had said at the Moscow summit. A few days before the end of Reagan's presidency, a visitor stopped by the Oval Office to say goodbye. He asked if Reagan had ever met an evil person. "Well, no person. But I believe evil exists." Like an evil empire? "Yes." He paused. "It was evil until he—until this one man made all the difference."

10. "THAT MAGIC LINE"

When did the Cold War end? As Reagan left office, there was disagreement about whether the U.S.-Soviet rivalry was truly nearing its conclusion. Margaret Thatcher had declared flatly that the Cold War was over, pointing to Gorbachev's steps toward demilitarization and his popularity in Western Europe. But not everyone was convinced. "The Cold War is not over," said the incoming national security adviser, Brent Scowcroft. "You have to define for me what you mean by Cold War," the new president, George H. W. Bush, said. Both remained uncertain whether Gorbachev had the support in the Kremlin to carry out his reforms, even if he wanted to. And they doubted his willingness to give up control of Eastern Europe. Bush's defense secretary was perhaps the most skeptical. "There are those who want to declare the Cold War over," Dick Cheney said. "I believe caution is in order. . . . We must guard against gambling our nation's security on what may be a temporary aberration."

Looking back on the final years of the Reagan presidency, different participants point to different events that indicated that the superpower conflict was effectively finished, even if leaders on both sides didn't perceive it at the time. George Shultz wrote that as early as 1985, Washington and Moscow "were smack in the middle" of the endgame of the Cold War. Gorbachev called the summit at

Reykjavik in 1986 the critical "breakthrough," the moment when the world saw "an agreement was possible." Interviewed twenty years after Reagan's speech at the Brandenburg Gate, John Whitehead said that, in his mind, "the Cold War was over" by the time Reagan went to Berlin. "Perestroika was rampant and the discussions we were having with the Soviets were very friendly. We'd won the day. We were making so much progress that if it wasn't formally over, the substance of it was."

No single event, taken in isolation, caused the Cold War to end. To paraphrase Gorbachev's letter to Reagan, the final years of the Cold War were a moving stream, the currents of history flowing in directions both unpredictable and unforeseen. Reagan and Gorbachev did not anticipate that the dialogue they began in Geneva would ultimately produce the earthshaking events of 1989. They may not have grasped the velocity of the changes that they unleashed, or anticipated how quickly the frustrations of millions of people would boil over. But the old order was dying. And sooner than most could have imagined, the enduring symbol of a divided world was gone.

The first stirrings of change came in Poland. There the communists' epic mismanagement of the economy had left the country mired in debt. The government's attempts to reduce it caused rampant inflation and soaring consumer prices. In protest, the underground workers' movement organized work stoppages across the country. Only a few years earlier, the country's leaders had responded to similar protests by declaring martial law. Now, knowing that Moscow would not back a resort to force, the authorities had no choice but to negotiate with the workers. After months of "roundtable" talks between the government and Lech Walesa, the leader of the opposition, the parties agreed in April 1989 to free elections for the National Assembly. Two months later, the communists lost all but one contested seat.

In Hungary, the most Western-oriented nation in the Warsaw Pact, the clamor for change came from young communist reformers, who patterned themselves after Gorbachev and forced the removal of János Kádár, the strongman who had ruled the country for three decades. The new party leaders announced that they would recognize the right to free speech and open the political system to opposition parties. In May, they removed the electrified fence that separated Hungary from Austria. Thousands of East Germans flooded into the country on "vacation," with no intention of going back. Some continued traveling west into Austria and for the first time encountered no resistance at the border. The Iron Curtain had begun to crumble.

The Bush administration watched the events in Eastern Europe with both excitement and apprehension. The new team had decided to pressure Gorbachev to let go of Moscow's satellites. "I thought the principal goal should be to try to lift the Kremlin's military boot from the necks of East Europeans," Scowcroft later said. Inside the administration, there was disagreement over the utility of continuing Reagan's personal diplomacy with Gorbachev. "This is one of the little kept secrets," says Condoleezza Rice, at the time the NSC's top Soviet specialist. "When we came in in January 1989 we thought Reagan had gone too far. We came in more suspicious of Gorbachev and Soviet motives and whether the change was real. But by April or May it was pretty clear that something real was happening." James Baker, Bush's secretary of state, says that the Bush team wanted "a bit of a pause in our relationship with the Soviet Union. That was done not so much because we were worried that the Reagan administration had gone too far too fast—although there were some who might have argued that. We did primarily because it was important to put George Bush's imprimatur on the nation's foreign policy."

Bush believed the United States should be tougher with the Soviets and hold them accountable if they failed to reduce their military presence and permit self-determination in Eastern Europe. He wanted to see results. "Promises are never enough," he said in a commencement speech at Texas A&M in May. And yet like Reagan, this president was more inclined than some of his aides to view Gorbachev's peace overtures as genuine. Bush didn't want to be seen as a hard-liner. In late May, when his speechwriters gave him the text of remarks he was to give at the Coast Guard Academy, Bush rejected it and told Scowcroft to start over. "He was tired of criticism casting him as stuck in a Cold War rut," Scowcroft said. "He felt the draft was bombastic, hard-line and full of 'macho' Cold War expressions that did not ring true to him."

Bush traveled to Europe in late May for a NATO summit. The centerpiece of the trip was a speech at the Rheingoldhalle in Mainz, Germany, the ancient city on the banks of the Rhine. The draft had been written by Mark Davis, a former journalist who handled many of Bush's foreign policy speeches. The day before the speech, Davis inadvertently erased it from his computer, forcing the speechwriting team to compose it again from memory. For the first time as president, Bush invoked the oppressive structure that his predecessor had challenged Gorbachev to tear down. "Nowhere is the division between East and West seen more clearly than in Berlin. And there this brutal Wall cuts neighbor from neighbor, brother from brother. . . . That Wall must come down." Bush cited the removal of barriers between Hungary and the West. "Let Berlin be next," he said.

On the surface, Berlin had changed little in the two years since Reagan had visited. In April, two months after border guards had gunned down a twenty-year-old who ventured too close to the Wall, the East German government secretly lifted its shoot-to-kill orders, though they refused to remove the latticework of spikes, barbed wire, watch towers, and alarms that still ringed the eastern side of the Wall. Such cosmetic symbols of the regime's authority, however, could not conceal the growing mood of discontent.

The Honecker government's attempts to crush the dissident move-ment—raiding churches, rounding up intellectuals, and employing Stasi agents to inform on their neighbors—only called more atten-tion to it. Underground reports on the government's repressive tac-tics began to spread beyond Berlin. "We had been isolated before," says Gerd Poppe. "But we built a network, an exchange throughout the country. It developed to a point where if there was an arrest in one place, we could diffuse it throughout East Germany through telephone and newspapers." Poppe and his fellow dissidents orga-nized lectures, marches, sit-ins, and candlelight vigils. Their move-ment grew.

Gorbachev watched the situation in East Germany with con-cern. He did not want to see the East German government col-lapse, but neither was he inclined to intervene to save it. Over the years he had tried with little effect to convince Honecker to liberal-ize. "It was as if I had been speaking to a brick wall," he wrote. Gor-bachev realized it was futile to resist the tide of rebellion against the regime; the East German people were voting with their feet. In Prague, some ten thousand East Germans sought asylum at the West German embassy, climbing over the gates of the embassy and pitching tents in the garden. They refused to leave. The Honecker government finally announced the refugees would be "expelled" to West Germany and their citizenship withdrawn. In an attempt to humiliate the refugees, he insisted that they be loaded onto sealed trains and transported west via the GDR. The move backfired. Throngs of East Germans turned out to cheer the trains as they rolled through the countryside; many tried to jump aboard.

By September 1989, some sixty thousand more East Germans had fled to Hungary. Gorbachev told the Hungarian communists that if they wanted to formally open their border with Austria, enabling citizens of the GDR to defect there, he would not object. In the seventy-two hours after the Hungarians announced that any Germans in Hungary would be allowed to enter Austria, 22,000 crossed the border to seek freedom in the West. Thousands more East Germans poured into Hungary.

A few weeks later Gorbachev went to Berlin. A delegation of Soviet officials had returned from East Germany and reported that Honecker was running out of time. "It's five minutes to midnight," they told Gorbachev. As Gorbachev drove into the city with Honecker for ceremonies commemorating the fortieth anniversary of the GDR, lines of young Germans along the route chanted "Gorbachev! Gorbachev!" That night he and Honecker watched a torchlight parade along the Unter den Linden by thousands of young Communist Party activists from all over the country. As they passed the viewing stand, the youths chanted, "Gorbachev, save us once more!" The anti-government vehemence of the young Germans—ostensibly supporters of the regime—stunned Gorbachev and the other foreign dignitaries in attendance. "This is the end," one of them said. Before leaving the city, Gorbachev made one final plea to Honecker and his comrades. "Life punishes those who delay," he told them. "As I understand it, life demands that you make courageous decisions."

It was too late. The protests against the government swelled. In Leipzig, ninety thousand people joined a demonstration calling for change; the next week, 300,000 showed up. "We are the people," was their rallying cry. When Honecker began to talk of using force against the protesters, members of his government finally rebelled, ousting Honecker on October 18 and installing Egon Krenz as the new party chief. Krenz flew to Moscow to ask Gorbachev for assistance to help pay off the country's massive foreign debt. He told Gorbachev that "measures should be taken to prevent any attempt at mass breakthrough" at the Berlin Wall. But Gorbachev said Soviet troops would not participate in any crackdown in Berlin. Three days later, 500,000 people took to the streets of East Berlin to demand free elections.

The government of Czechoslovakia opened its border, and

thirty thousand Germans left the country in forty-eight hours. The pressure on the government had become irresistible. The cabinet resigned en masse, followed by the Politburo. On the evening of November 9, a government spokesman named Günther Schabowski announced that the GDR had decided to issue travel visas to any citizen who wanted to leave the country. The idea was to allow East Germans to emigrate directly to West Germany, without going through third countries. Krenz wanted to phase the new rules in gradually, but when a reporter asked Schabowski when they would come into effect, Schabowski said, "So far as I know, that is, immediate. Without delay." Within an hour, the Associated Press reported that "the GDR is opening its borders." West German television networks picked up the news. "The gates of the Wall stand wide open," the state-run network ARD reported.

By 11:30 P.M., crowds had gathered at the checkpoint at Bornholmer Strasse and were pushing forward. At first border police actually tried to check passports, then realized it was futile. The masses surged through. Many of them ran. Crowds of West Berliners waited on the other side, hugging strangers and popping champagne. By midnight all of the checkpoints along the Wall were opened. That night some fifty thousand people streamed across and tens of thousands more rushed to join them, including a young physicist named Angela Merkel, who was at her weekly appointment at an East Berlin sauna when the Wall came down.

Christian Halbrock, who two years earlier had participated in the anti-government demonstrations on the eve of Ronald Reagan's visit, was told by a friend that the borders were open. "I thought I'd try to go, but it must be a mistake." He got to the border, showed a guard his passport and walked into another world. He had never been to West Berlin. "We were in a quiet residential neighborhood," he says, "but we thought it was like Vegas." He stopped an elderly man and asked him where to go, what he should see, but the man shrugged. He was from East Berlin too. Halbrock spent the night talking to anyone he encountered. He didn't go home until the next day. Gerd Poppe was visiting another dissident's home when he looked out the window and noticed the road jammed with a line of Trabants, all going one way. "Switch on the TV," he said. "Something's going on." East German television was showing the first images of people crossing the checkpoints. Poppe headed there too. Later that night he walked into West Berlin, his first trip outside East Germany in twenty-eight years.

Bush was in the Oval Office when Scowcroft told him that there were reports of people crossing the Berlin Wall. They turned on a television to see live coverage of the celebrations in the city. Condoleezza Rice received a call at her office from an aide to Robert Gates, Scowcroft's deputy. "The president wants you over here right away," the aide said. "He wants to know what in the world is going on in Berlin." But Rice didn't know either. "Turn on CNN!" the aide said. Rice did. "There they were, carving up the Wall," she recalls.

Marlin Fitzwater, the White House press secretary, wanted Bush to issue a statement, but the president refused. "I'm not going to dance on the Berlin Wall," he said. He didn't want to provoke the Soviets and embarrass Gorbachev by claiming victory, but agreed to meet with a few reporters to talk about the unfolding events. Lesley Stahl of CBS asked him why he seemed so subdued. "This is a great victory for our side," she said, "but you don't seem elated." "I'm not an emotional kind of guy," Bush said. Stahl pressed him again. Why wasn't he elated? "I'm very pleased," the president finally said. Though the president insisted on stoicism, his aides quietly celebrated. At the State Department, James Baker was hosting a lunch for Corazon Aquino, the president of the Philippines, when an aide handed him a note saying the Berlin Wall was open. Baker stood up and read the note to the table. Then he and his guests drank a champagne toast.

Bush spoke to Chancellor Kohl the next day. Berlin was "an enormous fair. It has the atmosphere of a festival," Kohl reported.

In a speech in Berlin he had thanked the United States for its part in bringing down the Wall. The crowd applauded. "Without the U.S. this day would not have been possible," Kohl said. "Tell your people that." Bush assured him that his aides would avoid "hot rhetoric that might by mistake cause a problem." Kohl also spoke with Gorbachev, who was struggling to make sense of the events in Berlin. "We are experiencing a historic turn toward new relations, to a new world," Gorbachev told Kohl. The mood of jubilation had given rise to talk of unifying Germany, East and West, and Gorbachev wanted to douse it. He believed that reforms could save the GDR. "We should not allow ourselves . . . to push the developments toward an unpredictable course, toward chaos, by forcing events. It would be undesirable." Kohl said he valued his relationship with Gorbachev. But he demurred about preserving the East German regime. The people would decide.

The fall of the Berlin Wall and the democratic revolutions that swept across Eastern Europe in 1989 were Gorbachev's greatest achievements. As communist power crumbled in country after country, he resisted the temptation to use force to stop it, as his predecessors might have done. "Employing force would clash with his overriding goal of transforming the image of the Soviet Union in the West," the historian Melvyn Leffler wrote. "He was seeking to build a common European home where the rules . . . required respect for the will of the residents." In the defining hour, Gorbachev's restraint convinced those around him of his greatness as a leader. "The Berlin Wall has collapsed. This entire era in the history of the socialist system is over," Gorbachev's aide Anatoly Chernyaev wrote in his diary the day after the Wall came down. "This is what Gorbachev has done. . . . He has sensed the pace of history and helped history to find a natural channel."

And yet by allowing Eastern Europe to go its own way, Gorbachev had unwittingly set in motion the events that would doom the Soviet empire. For some Russians, the fall of the Berlin Wall was anything but a cause for celebration; instead it came to be seen as a moment of humiliating national impotence. In the days after the Wall collapsed, Vladimir Putin and his fellow KGB agents in Dresden burned so many of their files, containing the names of secret agents and operations, that the furnace burst. At one point a mob of Germans besieged the KGB office, prompting Putin to call for support from Soviet troops stationed nearby. They did not come. The Soviets' virtual surrender shocked Putin, fueling his desire to someday restore Russia to its rightful place on the world stage. "The country no longer existed," he said later. "It disappeared."

In 1990, Gorbachev was awarded the Nobel Peace Prize. *Time* named him the Man of the Decade, the first time the magazine had ever conferred such an honor. And yet as his standing abroad soared, Gorbachev's fortunes at home began to plummet. His economic reforms stalled, while political opponents used their new freedoms to denounce the man who had introduced them. Moscow's grip on the Baltic states, home to millions of Russian minorities, was beginning to weaken. Bowing to inevitability, Gorbachev assented to German unification and, in May 1990, to German membership in NATO. Scowcroft said that "the Cold War ended when the Soviets accepted a united Germany in NATO." That was the final straw for hard-liners in the Kremlin, who staged a coup in August 1991, detaining Gorbachev for three days at his summer home in the Crimea. Though he quickly regained control, Gorbachev's political authority was gone. Led by Boris Yeltsin, the president of the Russian Republic, clamor for dissolution of the Soviet Union became impossible to resist. The old regime collapsed. On Christmas Day 1991, Gorbachev resigned as president of the USSR. He never held office again.

A few days after the collapse of the Berlin Wall, Lou Cannon met Reagan in the former president's office on the top floor of the Fox

Plaza in Century City, California. Cannon was working on a biography of Reagan, *The Role of a Lifetime*. Their conversation turned to the events in Berlin. "Did you expect this to happen?" Cannon asked. Reagan shrugged. "Someday," he said.

The fall of the Berlin Wall led to reappraisals of Reagan and his speech at the Brandenburg Gate. For two years, the speech had been little more than a footnote to history. On the night of November 9, however, all three network newscasts replayed footage of Reagan's challenge to Gorbachev in their reports on the Wall's collapse. "[President Kennedy] and every President since called for [the Wall] to be torn down," ABC's Peter Jennings said. "None more eloquently than President Reagan, two years ago." That network's *Prime Time Live* opened its broadcast with the "Tear Down This Wall" clip.

Sam Donaldson interviewed Reagan in Century City. "When you stood in front of the Wall—and we've shown those pictures tonight—and you challenged, 'Mr. Gorbachev, tear down this Wall,' did you think it would come this soon?" Donaldson asked. "I didn't know when it would come, but I have to tell you, I'm an eternal optimist," Reagan said. "I believed with all my heart that it was in the future." As Donaldson tried to wrap up the interview— "President Reagan, you're looking well! We're glad to see it!"— Reagan interjected. "Could I just finish with one thing?" he said. He then recalled how, on that day in Berlin, he had looked across the Wall and had seen the East German police preventing people "from getting anywhere near the Wall, to keep them from hearing, overhearing anything that we might be saying on the other side, on the west side of that Wall. So there was another sign of their system and how it worked with their own people."

There is little evidence that any such commotion took place in East Berlin on the day of the speech, or that Reagan was at any point in a position to see it. But Reagan never allowed the facts to get in the way of a great story.

Scarcely noted by most of the world when it was actually delivered, the "Tear Down This Wall" speech came to be inextricably associated with the defining historical event of the late twentieth century. It entered American lore. In his Thanksgiving address to the nation two weeks after the Wall came down, Bush praised the American presidents who had defended Berlin's freedom: Truman in the 1940s, Eisenhower in the 1950s, Kennedy in the 1960s, and Nixon, Ford, and Carter in the 1970s. "And in the 1980s," Bush said, "Ronald Reagan went to Berlin to say: Tear down this Wall!" To Berliners, Reagan's speech was a clarion expression of the American commitment to their freedom. When the Reagans visited Berlin in September 1990, en route to see Gorbachev in Moscow, modest crowds came out to greet Reagan and shake his hand. "The Man Who Made Those Pussyfooters and Weaklings Feel Ashamed," read the headline of one German newspaper. Slowed by age and straining to hear questions shouted at him, Reagan nevertheless accepted a photographer's challenge and took a hammer to the Wall, knocking out a few chips of concrete. "Ronnie, we thank you!" one woman shouted in German. "We can't be happy until the whole world knows freedom the way we do," Reagan said.

Less than a month later, the two Germanys were formally reunited. Berlin celebrated again. "There were one million people here last night at the very spot where the Wall used to stand," Kohl told Bush in a three-minute phone call, "where President Reagan called on Mr. Gorbachev to open this gate." The German chancellor had been with Reagan that day; on the crowning night of Kohl's career, he still thought of Reagan's speech. "Words can't describe the feeling," he said.

The end of the Cold War marked the start of a period of global economic growth that would last for nearly two decades. The number of democracies in the world nearly doubled between 1989 and 2009. The collapse of communism did not, however, signal the end of history, in Francis Fukuyama's memorable phrase. As Soviet power receded, the United States faced new challenges to its military and economic power, from radical Islam and a rising China. In some former Eastern Bloc countries, including Russia itself, the depredations of socialism gave way to a form of boom-and-bust capitalism that produced a new class of oligarchs but left millions unprepared to succeed in a market economy. And yet the end of the U.S.-Soviet conflict, the liberalization of Eastern Europe and the removal of the specter of nuclear war made the world a better, safer, and saner place. None would have been possible without Gorbachev; in this drama, Reagan was the supporting actor.

"Reagan had not 'won' the Cold War in the fashion that American conservatives later claimed," James Mann concluded in his book *The Rebellion of Ronald Reagan*. "Rather Gorbachev had abandoned the field." Still, Mann lauds Reagan for giving Gorbachev the "breathing room" to remake Soviet policy, by convincing him that the United States had no interest in perpetuating conflict. Most other scholars share that view. The liberal historian Sean Wilentz, who is critical of Reagan's record on domestic policy, wrote in 2008 that Reagan's "success in helping finally to end the cold war is one of the greatest achievements by any president of the United States—and arguably the greatest single achievement since 1945."

How much did Reagan's speech at the Brandenburg Gate contribute to that achievement? What role did it play in bringing down the Berlin Wall and ending the Cold War? Few presidential speeches produce immediate, tangible change. Even the most inspiring orations rarely inspire listeners to take action. No one would claim that merely by calling on Gorbachev to tear down the Wall, Reagan convinced him to do it. After all, it was not Gorbachev who brought about the Wall's collapse. It crumbled from its own weight. Like the regime that built it and the political system that it symbolized, the Wall met its ignominious end because it attempted to deprive people of their most basic aspirations. Ultimately, as Reagan predicted, the Wall could not withstand freedom. Reagan's speech did presciently identify Berlin as the proving ground of Gorbachev's intentions. If Gorbachev sought peace and liberalization, then he should let the Wall come down. In the end, he did.

"Tear Down This Wall"'s significance lies less in the outcomes it directly led to than in the ideas it represented. It was on the right side of history. Reagan did not expect Gorbachev to open the Brandenburg Gate simply because Reagan challenged him to do so. But throughout his presidency—throughout his life—Reagan did cling to the view that the world need not remain divided, that people could overcome the barriers between them, that change was possible. That's what allowed him to work with Gorbachev to find a way out of the Cold War. And perhaps as much as any statement Reagan made as president, "Tear Down This Wall" crystallized that core belief. As George Shultz described it, "There were people who thought the Soviet Union would never change—'We're here, they're there, that's life. The name of the game is coexistence.' And those people thought it was a mistake for President Reagan and me to be dealing with them the way we were. Ronald Reagan challenged that. His view never changed—the Soviet Union was corrupt and immoral. Economically that system just couldn't work for a long time. So sooner or later it would change. If you went to Berlin, and you looked at that Wall, it looked like it would be there forever. But to go there and say 'Tear down this Wall' was a statement that things could change. It was a metaphor for that."

For nearly ten years, Peter Robinson did not talk about his involvement in the "Tear Down This Wall" speech. He left the White House in 1988 to attend Stanford Business School and married Edita Piedra, another former Reagan staffer. He worked at Rupert Murdoch's News Corp. and at the Securities and Exchange Commission. One day in 1997, Robinson came across a German newspaper article about the new U.S. ambassador to Germany—John

Kornblum. Robinson had met him on the advance trip in 1987, when Kornblum was the ranking diplomat in West Berlin; as Robinson remembered, Kornblum had advised him not to mention the Wall in his speech. To Robinson's amazement, the German article now gave Kornblum credit for authoring Reagan's Brandenburg Gate speech.

"It made me cross," Robinson says. He mentioned his dismay to John Podhoretz, a former Bush speechwriter who had founded a new conservative magazine, *The Weekly Standard.* The tenth anniversary of the speech was coming up, Podhoretz told Robinson. Why don't you write about it? "That was the first time I said anything in public, ten years after the event," Robinson says. "That's when it came back into my life." It never left. Robinson gave further details of his role in the speech in two memoirs, the second called *How Ronald Reagan Changed My Life.* On the fifteenth anniversary of the speech, he went back to Berlin and re-created the dinner party at the Elzes, as part of a one-hour Fox News special. Today he works out of an office at the Hoover Institution on the Stanford University campus, a few doors down from George Shultz and Condoleezza Rice. He could not have known twenty years ago that his professional life would forever be defined by those four words spoken by Ronald Reagan in Berlin. "'Oh yeah, you know Peter, he's the one who wrote . . .' when I meet somebody new that's how I'm introduced," he says. Such introductions are "perfectly standard . . . and rather grating after a while."

After his sojourn into West Berlin the night the Wall came down, Gerd Poppe returned home. He didn't sit still. He continued to publish articles criticizing the communists and exposing their crimes. When the East German regime finally crumbled, Poppe was a delegate at the roundtable talks about the future of Germany; after unification, he was elected to the Bundestag as a member of the Green Party. In 1992 Poppe was among the first East Germans to view the files the Stasi had secretly kept on six million citizens, one-third of the country's population. Poppe's file was ten thousand pages long and contained personal letters he had never received, pictures taken through the window of his apartment, and transcripts of taped telephone calls. It revealed that the government had for years attempted to break up his marriage, which ended in 1997. The following year, Poppe became the German government's high commissioner for human rights, a position that allowed him to travel abroad widely, an opportunity the communists had denied him for nearly thirty years. Today, he lives in Prenzlauer Berg, in what used to be East Berlin. The walls of his home are stacked high with books, newspapers, and an impressive collection of jazz CDs. On one shelf sit two dozen black three-ring binders containing copies of Poppe's entire Stasi file, a reminder of the years he lived and lost.

Svetlana Savranskaya graduated from Moscow State University in 1988. The Russian people were transforming themselves, breaking free of the shackles that had restrained them for a generation, rediscovering the world. It was an exhilarating time. "I remember feeling like I could say or do anything," she says. She was accepted into the doctoral program in political science at Emory University in Atlanta. After years of studying the U.S. political system from afar, she found that she knew more about it than many of her American classmates. She became a research fellow at the National Security Archive at George Washington University, where she has helped unearth, translate, and publish thousands of documents from the archives of the former Soviet Union. One of the country's leading authorities on the end of the Cold War, Savranskaya had never publicly detailed her own role as a witness to history until I met her in her office in Washington. Her story is testament to how quickly the world can change: prevented by the KGB from even catching a glimpse of Ronald Reagan in Berlin, she shook the president's hand in Moscow one year later. "I kind of feel that it was really symbolic somehow," she says, "that I was there."

Ronald Reagan and Mikhail Gorbachev met one last time, at Reagan's ranch in the Santa Barbara Mountains. It was the summer of 1992; both men were out of power. The world had moved on. Reagan drove Gorbachev around the grounds of the 630-acre ranch and gave him a cowboy hat. Gorbachev put it on backward, to Reagan's delight. "This will be more famous than the picture of the two of us in front of the fireplace in Geneva," Gorbachev said. The next day they went to the Reagan Library in Simi Valley, and posed in front of a slab of the Berlin Wall, donated to the library by Carl Karcher, the fast-food magnate. Reagan presented Gorbachev with the first Ronald Reagan Freedom Award. He draped a medal around Gorbachev's neck. Gorbachev hugged him. "We were able to make a difference," Gorbachev said.

They never saw each other again. By that time, Reagan's health had begun to deteriorate. He was frail, easily disoriented and sometimes unaware of the presence of others in the room. After a time, his security detail at Rancho del Cielo told Reagan he could no longer ride horses. In 1994, during Reagan's annual checkup at the Mayo Clinic, doctors diagnosed Reagan with Alzheimer's disease. On November 5, he composed a two-page, handwritten letter disclosing his illness: "I intend to live the remainder of the years God gives me on this earth doing the things I have always done," he wrote.

"In closing, let me thank you, the American people for giving me the great honor of allowing me to serve as your President. When the Lord calls me home whenever that may be, I will leave with the greatest love for this country of ours and eternal optimism for its future. I now begin the journey that will lead me into the sunset of my life. I know that for America there will always be a bright dawn ahead."

The former president faded away. He made no more public appearances but continued to go to his office in Century City, where he received visits from former aides, supporters, and friends, most of whom he no longer recognized. Peter Hannaford, who had worked with Reagan since the 1970s and accompanied him on his first trip to Berlin, recalls visiting Reagan in 1996. "I could tell he knew me but he wasn't quite sure where to place me in his firmament," Hannaford says. Reagan pulled a ceramic replica of the Capitol off the shelf. Whoever had decorated the office had put it on the top shelf; Reagan asked that it be lowered to eye level. "Well, that's a good idea," Hannaford said. "Now everyone can see it." "Yes," Reagan replied. "You know, it's our national building." Reagan could no longer remember what the building was called. As he said goodbye for the last time, Hannaford thought, "This guy's a trouper. He's struggling with this disease and yet when he sees people he's known he wants to rise to the occasion. He wants at least to make you think he's understanding everything you're talking about, whether he is or not."

In December 1995, Reagan's daughter, Patti Davis, wrote in her diary that "my mother and I acknowledge that we both fear this will be my father's last Christmas." He lived through eight more, though he was all but comatose during the last years of his life. He died on June 5, 2004, his eyes opening a final time to see Nancy before he stopped breathing. The next week was filled with televised tributes to Reagan and twenty-four-hour cable news coverage of the funeral proceedings, scripted by former members of the White House advance team. Hundreds of thousands of Americans filed past the flag-covered casket in California and Washington, where the former president lay in state for two days. The clip of "Tear Down This Wall" was replayed dozens of times. That single phrase in Berlin seemed to capture the essence of Reagan: a clear, simple, resolute message of optimism that sounded all the more appealing at a time when America's image had been tarnished by a divisive war in Iraq. "It made the American public feel he was a better president," said John Whitehead. "It was so typical of Reagan to come up with a simple, radical, dramatic sentence, and this was the primary example of that: Mr. Gorbachev, tear down this Wall. It was that magic line."

Gorbachev traveled to Washington to pay his respects to Reagan. He was seventy-three years old. His wife, Raisa, had died in 1999 from leukemia. In his own country, Gorbachev was a forgotten man, blamed for the dismemberment of the Soviet empire and repudiated by supporters of Russia's president, Vladimir Putin. But in Washington Gorbachev basked in some of the adulation he had enjoyed seventeen years earlier, when he got out of his limousine to shake hands with locals on Connecticut Avenue. "It was a wonderful encounter," he recalled. He was still feisty and contentious, challenging one reporter's suggestion that Reagan had won the Cold War. "That's not serious. I think we all lost the Cold War. We only won when the Cold War ended." Reagan had decided to become a peacemaker at the right time, Gorbachev said. "He was a person committed to certain values and traditions. For him the American dream was not just rhetoric. It was something he felt in his heart."

Reagan recognized that dream as one not limited to Americans, but an aspiration shared by millions throughout the world. He never stopped believing he could help them realize it. The future belongs to the free, he often said. And even walls fall down.

EPILOGUE

On July 24, 2008, Barack Obama spoke to a crowd of 200,000 people in Berlin. Obama was making his first overseas trip as the presumptive Democratic nominee for president, one that would also take him to London, Paris, Jerusalem, Amman, Baghdad, and Kabul. His speech in Berlin was not without controversy. Two weeks before he arrived, German newspapers reported that Angela Merkel, the German chancellor, had rebuffed the Obama campaign's request to deliver the speech near the Brandenburg Gate, as Ronald Reagan had twenty-one years earlier. (Merkel's spokesman said it would be "odd" for an American presidential candidate to give a speech there, before he had been elected.) Obama ultimately settled on a site in front of the Victory Column, the 230-foot-high Prussian-era monument located in the Tiergarten. Though Obama's young speechwriters often borrowed from John F. Kennedy's rhetoric, it was Reagan whom Obama most conciously echoed in Berlin. "When you, the German people, tore down that Wall—a Wall that divided East and West, freedom and tyranny, fear and hope—walls came tumbling down around the world." The "greatest danger" of the twenty-first century would be to allow new walls to divide the world again. "The walls between races and tribes; natives and immigrants; Christian and Muslim and Jew cannot stand," Obama said. "These now are the walls we must tear down."

As a candidate, Obama often spoke of his admiration for Reagan. In one interview in early 2008, he said that Reagan's presidency had a greater impact on the country than did Bill Clinton's—a remark for which he was attacked by his Democratic primary opponents. "Ronald Reagan changed the trajectory of America. . . . He tapped into what people were already feeling, which is: we want clarity, we want optimism, we want a return to that sense of dynamism and entrepreneurship that had been missing." In his 2006 book *The Audacity of Hope*, Obama criticized the Reagan administration for waging an "assault on the poor" and ignoring "sources of misery in the world" beyond communism. But Obama also wrote that he felt far more affinity for Reagan's approach to foreign policy than did most liberals. "Pride in our country, respect for our armed services, a healthy appreciation for the dangers beyond our borders, an insistence that there was no easy equivalence between East and West—in all this I had no quarrel with Reagan," he wrote. "And when the Berlin Wall came down, I had to give the old man his due, even if I never gave him my vote."

Though vastly different in their political philosophies, the fortieth and forty-fourth presidents also have much in common. Both had strained relationships with their fathers. Both catapulted themselves to national prominence with electrifying speeches on behalf of losing presidential candidates (Reagan's "A Time for Choosing" speech during the 1964 Goldwater campaign; Obama's endorsement of John Kerry at the 2004 Democratic National Convention.) Both took office during times of economic crisis and spent the early months of their presidencies focused on passage of their domestic agendas. Both used their oratorical skills to connect with the American people and project an aura of even-keeled confidence, openness, and optimism. Both could be said to possess what Oliver Wendell Holmes famously ascribed to Franklin Delano Roosevelt, a leader revered by both Reagan and Obama: a first-class temperament. Had the two presidents ever met, they might well have seen in the other a kindred spirit.

Obama's approach to the presidency does depart in significant ways from Reagan's. The financial meltdown of 2008 left the global economy teetering on the edge of a depression. In response, the Obama administration authorized a massive increase in federal spending and expanded the government's role in the health care system. Such initiatives would have repelled Reagan, who said in his first Inaugural Address, "Government isn't the solution to our problem—government *is* the problem." Like Reagan, Obama has been forced to deal with double-digit unemployment that has eroded his popularity. On the world stage, Obama adopted a less hawkish tone than Reagan did during his early years, by reaching out to the Islamic world, seeking partnership with rising powers like China and Russia, and signaling a desire for negotiations with Iran.

At the same time, Obama has also sought to revive one of Reagan's most cherished goals: the quest for a world free of nuclear weapons. In an April 2009 speech in Prague, Obama said, "This goal will not be reached quickly—perhaps not in my lifetime. It will take patience and persistence. But now we, too, must ignore the voices who tell us the world cannot change." A few weeks after Obama's speech, I met Mikhail Gorbachev in Rome, where he was speaking at a conference on nuclear security. Gorbachev has slowed with age, his once brisk gait now more like a deliberate shuffle, but he still brims with intellectual vitality. "President Obama started taking this position during the campaign," Gorbachev said. "It was received by knowledgeable people in Russia with great approval. It's a resumption, an attempt to do what [Reagan and I] were trying to do when we were moving in this challenging, difficult process of nuclear disarmament."

Obama can take cues from the examples of both Reagan and Gorbachev. Reagan's willingness to negotiate with Gorbachev angered and mystified many of his supporters, who viewed the Soviet Union as an implacable enemy and read the president's conciliatory gestures as evidence he had gone "soft" on communism. In fact, Reagan's core convictions—his belief in the superiority of capitalist societies over socialist ones, his faith in the fundamental desire for freedom, and his abhorrence for nuclear war—never changed. Unlike some who later laid claim to his legacy, however, he did not believe those values could be imposed on others by force. His rhetoric often sounded unyielding, but he nonetheless sought to avert conflict through personal diplomacy.

Reagan did not harbor illusions about what negotiations might produce. And yet even as he authorized huge increases in America's military budget, Reagan managed to convince Gorbachev that the Soviet Union had nothing to fear from the United States. In doing so Reagan provided his counterpart with the space to pursue the changes that ultimately undid communism and brought the Cold War to an end. To accomplish real change in international relations—as Reagan recognized and Obama may soon discover— a president cannot simply stand on principle and refuse to engage with adversaries. He must do both.

It remains to be seen whether Obama can achieve a rapprochement with a country such as Iran comparable to Reagan's breakthrough with the USSR. (There is no Gorbachev in Tehran, at least not yet.) The threats facing America cannot be willed away. Defusing them will require the mix of firm resolve and patient diplomacy practiced by successful American statesmen throughout the Cold War. It will also require a faith in the unseen, a conviction that even today's seemingly intractable conflicts can eventually be resolved. That need not be a prescription for naïveté. Reagan's gift was his ability to speak candidly about the realities of the age while still presenting an optimistic vision of the future. In his best speeches— most famously at the Brandenburg Gate—Reagan found a way both to defend American interests and make people believe in a more peaceful world. Obama's challenge, and that of his successors, will be to do the same.

NOTES ON SOURCES

ARCHIVES AND COLLECTIONS

This book draws on primary source materials held by the following:

Ronald Reagan Presidential Library and Museum, Simi Valley, California

The National Security Archive, George Washington University, Washington, D.C.

Reagan Oral History Project, Miller Center, University of Virginia, Charlottesville, Virginia

Vanderbilt Television News Archive, Vanderbilt University, Nashville, Tennessee

Bundesbeauftragte für die Unterlagen des Staatssicherheitsdienstes der ehemaligen Deutschen Demokratischen Republik (Federal Commissioner for the Records of the State Security Service of the former German Democratic Republic), Berlin

Staatsbibliothek zu Berlin—Preußischer Kulturbesitz (Berlin State Library—Prussian Cultural Heritage), Berlin

Archiv der DDR—Opposition (Archive of the GDR Opposition), Berlin

I received access to additional documents through the following:

State Department cables relating to the Brandenburg Gate speech and its aftermath, released by U.S. Department of State, through the Freedom of Information Act.

Full text of memcons between Ronald Reagan and Mikhail Gorbachev at their five summits and text of Reagan's June 12, 1987, telephone conversation with Margaret Thatcher, made available by the Margaret Thatcher Foundation (www.margaretthatcher.org).

The Reagan Diaries: The Complete Box Set, edited by Douglas Brinkley, courtesy of Douglas Brinkley.

Peter Robinson journal entries, courtesy of Peter Robinson.

William Henkel memo to Frank Carlucci and Donald Regan, February 3, 1987, and Thomas Reed letter to Ronald Reagan, March 25, 1987, courtesy of Wynton Hall.

Entries from Gerd Poppe's Stasi files, courtesy of Gerd Poppe.

PERIODICALS

The American Interest
The Atlantic
Die Welt
Frankfurter Allgemeine Zeitung
Los Angeles Times
New York Times
Newsweek
Sueddeutsche Zeitung
Time
Washington Post
The Weekly Standard

BOOKS

I am indebted to numerous historians, journalists, and former government officials who have written about Ronald Reagan, his presidency, and the end of the Cold War. Of particular value to me were biographies of Reagan by Lou Cannon, James Mann, Edmund Morris, Richard Reeves, and Sean Wilentz; Melvyn P. Leffler's study of the Cold War, *For the Soul of Mankind*; and Tony Judt's history of modern Europe, *Postwar*. This book is also informed by the following sources:

Anderson, Martin, and Annelise Anderson. *Reagan's Secret War: The Untold Story of His Fight to Save the World from Nuclear Disaster.* New York: Crown, 2009.

Brown, Archie. *The Gorbachev Factor.* Oxford: Oxford University Press, 1997.

Bush, George H. W. *Public Papers of the Presidents: 1989.* Washington, D.C.: Government Printing Office, 1990.

Bush, George, H. W. and Brent A. Scowcroft. *A World Transformed.* New York: Vintage, 1998.

Brinkley, Douglas. *The Boys of Pointe du Hoc: Ronald Reagan, D-Day, and the U.S. Army 2nd Ranger Battalion.* New York: William Morrow, 2005.

Cannon, Lou. *President Reagan: The Role of a Lifetime.* New York: Public Affairs, 2000.

Carter, Jimmy. *Public Papers of the Presidents: 1979.* Washington, D.C.: Government Printing Office, 1980.

Chernyaev, Anatoly. *My Six Years with Gorbachev.* Trans. and ed. by Robert D. English and Elizabeth Tucker. University Park: Pennsylvania State University Press, 2000.

Clarke, Thurston. *Ask Not: The Inauguration of John F. Kennedy and the Speech That Changed America.* New York: Henry Holt, 2004.

Dallek, Matthew. *The Right Moment: Ronald Reagan's First Victory and the Decisive Turning Point in American Politics.* New York: Free Press, 2000.

Dallek, Robert. *An Unfinished Life: John F. Kennedy, 1917–1963.* Boston: Little, Brown, 2003.

Daum, Andreas. *Kennedy in Berlin.* Cambridge: Cambridge University Press, 2007.

Davis, Patti. *The Long Goodbye.* New York: Alfred A. Knopf, 2004.

Deaver, Michael K. *A Different Drummer: My Thirty Years with Ronald Reagan.* New York: HarperCollins, 2001.

Diggins, John Patrick. *Ronald Reagan: Fate, Freedom and the Making of History.* New York: W.W. Norton, 2007.

Dobrynin, Anatoly. *In Confidence: Moscow's Ambassador to America's Six Cold War Presidents.* New York: Random House, 1995.

Eliot, Marc. *Reagan: The Hollywood Years.* New York: Harmony, 2008.

Evans, Thomas W. *The Education of Ronald Reagan: The General Electric Years and the Untold Story of His Conversion to Conservatism.* New York: Cambridge University Press, 2006.

Fitzgerald, Frances. *Way Out There in the Blue: Reagan, Star Wars and the End of the Cold War.* New York: Simon & Schuster, 2000.

Garton Ash, Timothy. *In Europe's Name: Germany and the Divided Continent.* New York: Vintage, 1994.

Gates, Robert M. *From the Shadows: The Ultimate Insider's Story of Five Presidents and How They Won the Cold War.* New York: Simon & Schuster, 1994.

Gorbachev, Mikhail. *Memoirs.* New York: Doubleday, 1995.

Holloway, David. *Stalin and the Bomb.* New Haven: Yale University Press, 1994.

Judt, Tony. *Postwar: A History of Europe Since 1945.* New York: Penguin, 2005.

Kengor, Paul. *The Crusader: Ronald Reagan and the Fall of Communism.* New York: Regan, 2006.

Kengor, Paul, and Patricia Clark Doerner. *The Judge: William P. Clark, Reagan's Top Hand.* San Francisco: Ignatius Press, 2007.

Kennedy, John F. *Public Papers of the Presidents: 1963.* Washington, D.C.: Government Printing Office, 1964.

Large, David Clay. *Berlin.* New York: Basic Books, 2000.

Leffler, Melvyn P. *For the Soul of Mankind: The United States, the Soviet Union and the Cold War.* New York: Hill & Wang, 2007.

———. *A Preponderance of Power: National Security, the Truman Administration and the Cold War.* Stanford: Stanford University Press, 1993.

Lettow, Paul. *Ronald Reagan and His Quest to Abolish Nuclear Weapons.* New York: Random House, 2005.

Mann, James. *The Rebellion of Ronald Reagan: A History of the End of the Cold War.* New York: Viking, 2009.

Matlock, Jack, Jr. *Reagan and Gorbachev: How the Cold War Ended.* New York: Random House, 2004.

McCullough, David. *Truman.* New York: Simon & Schuster, 1992.

Morris, Edmund. *Dutch: A Memoir of Ronald Reagan.* New York: Random House, 1999.

Naimark, Norman M. *The Russians in Germany.* Cambridge: Harvard University Press, 1994.

Nixon, Richard M. *Public Papers of the Presidents: 1969.* Washington, D.C.: Government Printing Office, 1970.

Noonan, Peggy. *What I Saw at the Revolution: A Political Life in the Reagan Era*. New York: Random House, 1990.

Parrish, Thomas. *Berlin in the Balance, 1945–1949: The Blockade, the Airlift, the First Major Battle of the Cold War*. Reading, Mass: Addison-Wesley, 1998.

Putin, Vladimir, and Natalie Gevorkyan, Natalya Timakova, and Andrei Kolesnikov. *First Person*. New York: Public Affairs, 2000.

Reagan, Nancy, with William Novak. *My Turn: The Memoirs of Nancy Reagan*. New York: Random House, 1989.

Reagan, Ronald. *An American Life*. New York: Simon & Schuster, 1990.

———. *Public Papers of the Presidents*: 1981, 1982, 1983, 1984, 1985, 1986, 1987, 1988. Washington, D.C.: Government Printing Office, 1982, 1983, 1984, 1985, 1986, 1987, 1988, 1989, 1990.

———. *Reagan: A Life in Letters*. Ed. Kiron K. Skinner, Annelise Anderson, and Martin Anderson. New York: Simon & Schuster, 2003.

———. *The Reagan Diaries*. Ed. Douglas Brinkley. New York: HarperCollins, 2007.

———. *Reagan in His Own Hand*. Ed. Kiron K. Skinner, Annelise Anderson, and Martin Anderson. New York: Simon & Schuster, 2001.

Reed, Thomas. *At the Abyss: An Insider's History of the Cold War*. New York: Ballantine, 2004.

Reeves, Richard. *President Kennedy: Profile of Power*. New York: Simon & Schuster, 1993.

———. *President Nixon: Alone in the White House*. New York: Simon & Schuster, 2001.

———. *President Reagan: The Triumph of the Imagination*. New York: Simon & Schuster, 2005.

Reynolds, David. *Summits: Six Meetings That Shaped the Twentieth Century*. New York: Basic Books, 2007.

Rhodes, Richard. *Arsenals of Folly: The Making of the Nuclear Arms Race*. New York: Alfred A. Knopf, 2007.

Richie, Alexandra. *Faust's Metropolis: A History of Berlin*. London: HarperCollins, 1998.

Robinson, Peter. *How Ronald Reagan Changed My Life*. New York: HarperCollins, 2003.

Schlesinger, Robert. *White House Ghosts: Presidents and Their Speechwriters*. New York: Simon & Schuster, 2008.

Schweizer, Peter. *Reagan's War: The Epic Story of His Forty-Year Struggle and Final Triumph over Communism*. New York: Anchor, 1997.

Shultz, George P. *Turmoil and Triumph: My Years as Secretary of State.* New York: Scribner, 1993.

Taylor, Frederick. *The Berlin Wall: A World Divided, 1961–1989.* New York: HarperCollins, 2007.

Trotnow, Helmut, and Florian Weiss, eds. *Tear Down This Wall: U.S. President Ronald Reagan at the Brandenburg Gate, June 12, 1987.* Berlin: Allied Museum, 2007.

Truman, Harry S. *Public Papers of the President: 1945.* Washington, D.C.: Government Printing Office, 1961.

Wapshott, Nicholas. *Ronald Reagan and Margaret Thatcher: A Political Marriage.* New York: Sentinel, 2007.

Wilentz, Sean. *The Age of Reagan: A History, 1974–2008.* New York: HarperCollins, 2008.

Zelikow, Philip, and Condoleezza Rice. *Germany Unified and Europe Transformed.* Cambridge: Harvard University Press, 1995.

INTERVIEWS

Howard Baker
James Baker
William Bodde
Leopold-Bill von Bredow
Douglas Brinkley
Richard Burt
Lou Cannon
Frank Carlucci
Eberhard Diepgen
Anthony Dolan
Ken Duberstein
Dieter Elz
Ingeborg Elz
Marlin Fitzwater
Josh Gilder
Tom Griscom
Peter Hannaford
Christian Halbrock

James Hooley
Clark Judge
John Kornblum
James Kuhn
Nelson Ledsky
Andrew Littlefair
James Matlock
Landon Parvin
Eva Quistorp
Condoleezza Rice
Peter Robinson
Peter Rodman
Dana Rohrabacher
Stephen Sestanovich
George Shultz
Richard von Weizsäcker
John Whitehead

APPENDIX

Remarks on East-West Relations at the Brandenburg Gate in West Berlin

JUNE 12, 1987

Thank you very much. Chancellor Kohl, Governing Mayor Diepgen, ladies and gentlemen:

Twenty four years ago, President John F. Kennedy visited Berlin, speaking to the people of this city and the world at the city hall. Well, since then two other presidents have come, each in his turn, to Berlin. And today I, myself, make my second visit to your city.

We come to Berlin, we American Presidents, because it's our duty to speak, in this place, of freedom. But I must confess, we're drawn here by other things as well: by the feeling of history in this city, more than 500 years older than our own nation; by the beauty of the Grunewald and the Tiergarten; most of all, by your courage and determination. Perhaps the composer, Paul Lincke, understood something about American Presidents. You see, like so many Presidents before me, I come here today because wherever I go, whatever I do: "Ich hab noch einen koffer in Berlin." [I still have a suitcase in Berlin.]

Our gathering today is being broadcast throughout Western Europe and North America. I understand that it is being seen and heard as well in the East. To those listening throughout Eastern Europe, I extend my warmest greetings and the good will of the

American people. To those listening in East Berlin, a special word: Although I cannot be with you, I address my remarks to you just as surely as to those standing here before me. For I join you, as I join your fellow countrymen in the West, in this firm, this unalterable belief: Es gibt nur ein Berlin. [There is only one Berlin.]

Behind me stands a wall that encircles the free sectors of this city, part of a vast system of barriers that divides the entire continent of Europe. From the Baltic, south, those barriers cut across Germany in a gash of barbed wire, concrete, dog runs, and guard-towers. Farther south, there may be no visible, no obvious wall. But there remain armed guards and checkpoints all the same—still a restriction on the right to travel, still an instrument to impose upon ordinary men and women the will of a totalitarian state. Yet it is here in Berlin where the wall emerges most clearly; here, cutting across your city, where the news photo and the television screen have imprinted this brutal division of a continent upon the mind of the world. Standing before the Brandenburg Gate, every man is a German, separated from his fellow men. Every man is a Berliner, forced to look upon a scar.

President von Weizsacker has said: "The German question is open as long as the Brandenburg Gate is closed." Today I say: As long as this gate is closed, as long as this scar of a wall is permitted to stand, it is not the German question alone that remains open, but the question of freedom for all mankind. Yet I do not come here to lament. For I find in Berlin a message of hope, even in the shadow of this wall, a message of triumph.

In this season of spring in 1945, the people of Berlin emerged from their air raid shelters to find devastation. Thousands of miles away, the people of the United States reached out to help. And in 1947 Secretary of State—as you've been told—George Marshall announced the creation of what would become known as the Marshall plan. Speaking precisely 40 years ago this month, he said:

"Our policy is directed not against any country or doctrine, but against hunger, poverty, desperation, and chaos."

In the Reichstag a few moments ago, I saw a display commemorating this 40th anniversary of the Marshall plan. I was struck by the sign on a burnt-out, gutted structure that was being rebuilt. I understand that Berliners of my own generation can remember seeing signs like it dotted throughout the Western sectors of the city. The sign read simply: "The Marshall plan is helping here to strengthen the free world." A strong, free world in the West, that dream became real. Japan rose from ruin to become an economic giant. Italy, France, Belgium—virtually every nation in Western Europe saw political and economic rebirth; the European Community was founded.

In West Germany and here in Berlin, there took place an economic miracle, the Wirtschaftswunder. Adenauer, Erhard, Reuter, and other leaders understood the practical importance of liberty—that just as truth can flourish only when the journalist is given freedom of speech, so prosperity can come about only when the farmer and businessman enjoy economic freedom. The German leaders reduced tariffs, expanded free trade, lowered taxes. From 1950 to 1960 alone, the standard of living in West Germany and Berlin doubled.

Where four decades ago there was rubble, today in West Berlin there is the greatest industrial output of any city in Germany-busy office blocks, fine homes and apartments, proud avenues, and the spreading lawns of park land. Where a city's culture seemed to have been destroyed, today there are two great universities, orchestras and an opera, countless theaters, and museums. Where there was want, today there's abundance—food, clothing, automobiles—the wonderful goods of the Ku'damm. From devastation, from utter ruin, you Berliners have, in freedom, rebuilt a city that once again ranks as one of the greatest on Earth. The Soviets may have had other plans. But, my friends, there were a few things the Soviets didn't count on Berliner herz, Berliner humor, ja, und Berliner schnauze. [Berliner heart, Berliner humor, yes, and a Berliner schnauze.] [Laughter]

In the 1950's, Khrushchev predicted: "We will bury you." But in the West today, we see a free world that has achieved a level of prosperity and well-being unprecedented in all human history. In the Communist world, we see failure, technological backwardness, declining standards of health, even want of the most basic kind-too little food. Even today, the Soviet Union still cannot feed itself. After these four decades, then, there stands before the entire world one great and inescapable conclusion: Freedom leads to prosperity. Freedom replaces the ancient hatreds among the nations with comity and peace. Freedom is the victor.

And now the Soviets themselves may, in a limited way, be coming to understand the importance of freedom. We hear much from Moscow about a new policy of reform and openness. Some political prisoners have been released. Certain foreign news broadcasts are no longer being jammed. Some economic enterprises have been permitted to operate with greater freedom from state control. Are these the beginnings of profound changes in the Soviet state? Or are they token gestures, intended to raise false hopes in the West, or to strengthen the Soviet system without changing it? We welcome change and openness; for we believe that freedom and security go together, that the advance of human liberty can only strengthen the cause of world peace.

There is one sign the Soviets can make that would be unmistakable, that would advance dramatically the cause of freedom and peace. General Secretary Gorbachev, if you seek peace, if you seek prosperity for the Soviet Union and Eastern Europe, if you seek liberalization: Come here to this gate! Mr. Gorbachev, open this gate! Mr. Gorbachev, tear down this wall!

I understand the fear of war and the pain of division that afflict this continent—and I pledge to you my country's efforts to help overcome these burdens. To be sure, we in the West must resist Soviet expansion. So we must maintain defenses of unassailable strength. Yet we seek peace; so we must strive to reduce arms on both sides. Beginning 10 years ago, the Soviets challenged the Western alliance with a grave new threat, hundreds of new and more deadly SS-20 nuclear missiles, capable of-striking every capital in Europe. The Western alliance responded by committing itself to a counterdeployment unless the Soviets agreed to negotiate a better solution; namely, the elimination of such weapons on both sides. For many months, the Soviets refused to bargain in earnestness. As the alliance, in turn, prepared to go forward with its counterdeployment, there were difficult days—days of protests like those during my 1982 visit to this city—and the Soviets later walked away from the table.

But through it all, the alliance held firm. And I invite those who protested then—I invite those who protest today—to mark this fact: Because we remained strong, the Soviets came back to the table. And because we remained strong, today we have within reach the possibility, not merely of limiting the growth of arms, but of eliminating, for the first time, an entire class of nuclear weapons from the face of the Earth. As I speak, NATO ministers are meeting in Iceland to review the progress of our proposals for eliminating these weapons. At the talks in Geneva, we have also proposed deep cuts in strategic offensive weapons. And the Western allies have likewise made far-reaching proposals to reduce the danger of conventional war and to place a total ban on chemical weapons.

While we pursue these arms reductions, I pledge to you that we will maintain the capacity to deter Soviet aggression at any level at which it might occur. And in cooperation with many of our allies, the United States is pursuing the Strategic Defense Initiative-research to base deterrence not on the threat of offensive retaliation, but on defenses that truly defend; on systems, in short, that will not target populations, but shield them. By these means we seek to increase the safety of Europe and all the world. But we must remember a crucial fact: East and West do not mistrust each other because we are armed; we are armed because we mistrust each other. And our differences are not about weapons but about liberty. When President Kennedy spoke at the City Hall those 24 years ago, freedom was encircled, Berlin was under siege. And today, despite all the pressures upon this city, Berlin stands secure in its liberty. And freedom itself is transforming the globe.

In the Philippines, in South and Central America, democracy has been given a rebirth. Throughout the Pacific, free markets are working miracle after miracle of economic growth. In the industrialized nations, a technological revolution is taking place—a revolution marked by rapid, dramatic advances in computers and telecommunications.

In Europe, only one nation and those it controls refuse to join the community of freedom. Yet in this age of redoubled economic growth, of information and innovation, the Soviet Union faces a choice: It must make fundamental changes, or it will become obsolete. Today thus represents a moment of hope. We in the West stand ready to cooperate with the East to promote true openness, to break down barriers that separate people, to create a safer, freer world.

And surely there is no better place than Berlin, the meeting place of East and West, to make a start. Free people of Berlin: Today, as in the past, the United States stands for the strict observance and full implementation of all parts of the Four Power Agreement of 1971. Let us use this occasion, the 750th anniversary of this city, to usher in a new era, to seek a still fuller, richer life for the Berlin of the future. Together, let us maintain and develop the ties between the Federal Republic and the Western sectors of Berlin, which is permitted by the 1971 agreement.

And I invite Mr. Gorbachev: Let us work to bring the Eastern and Western parts of the city closer together, so that all the inhabitants of all Berlin can enjoy the benefits that come with life in one of the great cities of the world. To open Berlin still further to all Europe, East and West, let us expand the vital air access to this city, finding ways of making commercial air service to Berlin more convenient, more comfortable, and more economical. We look to the day when West Berlin can become one of the chief aviation hubs in all central Europe.

With our French and British partners, the United States is prepared to help bring international meetings to Berlin. It would be only fitting for Berlin to serve as the site of United Nations meetings, or world conferences on human rights and arms control or other issues that call for international cooperation. There is no better way to establish hope for the future than to enlighten young minds, and we would be honored to sponsor summer youth exchanges, cultural events, and other programs for young Berliners from the East. Our French and British friends, I'm certain, will do the same. And it's my hope that an authority can be found in East Berlin to sponsor visits from young people of the Western sectors.

One final proposal, one close to my heart: Sport represents a source of enjoyment and ennoblement, and you many have noted that the Republic of Korea—South Korea—has offered to permit certain events of the 1988 Olympics to take place in the North. International sports competitions of all kinds could take place in both parts of this city. And what better way to demonstrate to the world the openness of this city than to offer in some future year to hold the Olympic games here in Berlin, East and West?

In these four decades, as I have said, you Berliners have built a great city. You've done so in spite of threats—the Soviet attempts to impose the East-mark, the blockade. Today the city thrives in spite of the challenges implicit in the very presence of this wall. What keeps you here? Certainly there's a great deal to be said for your fortitude, for your defiant courage. But I believe there's something deeper, something that involves Berlin's whole look and feel and way of life—not mere sentiment. No one could live long in Berlin without being completely disabused of illusions. Something instead, that has seen the difficulties of life in Berlin but chose to accept them, that continues to build this good and proud city in contrast to a surrounding totalitarian presence that refuses to release human energies or aspirations. Something that speaks with a powerful voice of affirmation, that says yes to this city, yes to the future, yes to freedom. In a word, I would submit that what keeps you in Berlin is love—love both profound and abiding.

Perhaps this gets to the root of the matter, to the most fundamental distinction of all between East and West. The totalitarian world produces backwardness because it does such violence to the spirit, thwarting the human impulse to create, to enjoy, to worship. The totalitarian world finds even symbols of love and of worship an affront. Years ago, before the East Germans began rebuilding their churches, they erected a secular structure: the television tower at Alexander Platz. Virtually ever since, the authorities have been working to correct what they view as the tower's one major flaw, treating the glass sphere at the top with paints and chemicals of every kind. Yet even today when the Sun strikes that sphere—that sphere that towers over all Berlin—the light makes the sign of the cross. There in Berlin, like the city itself, symbols of love, symbols of worship, cannot be suppressed.

As I looked out a moment ago from the Reichstag, that embodiment of German unity, I noticed words crudely spray-painted upon the wall, perhaps by a young Berliner, "This wall will fall. Beliefs become reality." Yes, across Europe, this wall will fall. For it cannot withstand faith; it cannot withstand truth. The wall cannot withstand freedom.

And I would like, before I close, to say one word. I have read, and I have been questioned since I've been here about certain demonstrations against my coming. And I would like to say just one thing, and to those who demonstrate so. I wonder if they have ever asked themselves that if they should have the kind of government they apparently seek, no one would ever be able to do what they're doing again.

Thank you and God bless you all.

ACKNOWLEDGMENTS

Like most presidential speeches, this book was a group effort. From the moment I first suggested the idea, Alice Mayhew championed, shaped, refined, and sustained it. Her sensitivity and wisdom are rightly treasured by all writers with whom she has worked. I am privileged to count myself among them.

This book would not exist but for the encouragement of my agent, David Halpern, to whom I am indebted for his unflagging friendship and counsel, as well as Chinese lunches too numerous to count. His colleague, Kathy Robbins, provided her support and sound advice from the outset.

I owe deep gratitude to three gifted researchers. Nadja Korinth not only tracked down German newspaper clippings and files from the Stasi archives but served as my guide around Berlin. Emily Feder helped set up interviews, organize documents, and check facts. While finishing her senior thesis at Princeton, Laura Fitzpatrick researched and wrote a camera-ready essay on the postwar history of Berlin, which formed the basis of the book's first chapter.

During my career at *Time* I've had the great and good fortune to work under three remarkable men. Walter Isaacson, a trusted mentor and friend for more than a decade, read the initial proposal for this book, pushed me to pursue it, and provided valuable suggestions on an early draft. Jim Kelly encouraged me to see the world and taught me much of what I know about writing and editing. Rick Stengel had the confidence to make me his deputy and allowed me to take leave to write this book, even when it meant less time for him to work on his own. A special thanks to the late Michael Kelly, whose work and example will forever inspire.

A number of people associated with the "Tear Down This Wall" speech gave of their time and spoke to me—none more generously than Peter Robinson, who sat for multiple interviews, guided me through the history of the speech, put me in contact with other sources, retrieved files from his days at the White House, and shared entries from his personal journal. I could not have embarked on this project, much less completed it, without his cooperation, for which he has my utmost appreciation.

Numerous scholars and archivists provided vital assistance and advice during my research. Wynton Hall shared two fascinating documents from Dick Wirthlin's papers. Douglas Brinkley gave me access to the full and unabridged *Reagan Diaries* a year before their publication in 2009. At the Ronald Reagan Presidential Library Sherrie Fletcher cheerfully guided me through the many boxes of papers on the speech housed there, tracked down missing documents, and gave me a tutorial on the ins and outs of the declassification process. In addition to sharing her extraordinary personal connection to Ronald Reagan, Svetlana Savranskaya pointed me to newly available material held at George Washington University's National Security Archive. Helmut Trotnow at the Allied Museum in Berlin offered reflections based on his research on Reagan's visit to Berlin. David Smith provided me with a place to work at that indispensable American institution, the New York Public Library.

At Simon & Schuster, Karen Thompson and Roger Labrie patiently helped guide this project to completion. A number of friends and colleagues also lent their support in ways large and small. Peter Beinart and Joel Stein read drafts of this book and offered sharp and insightful suggestions. Two colleagues from *Time*, Skye Gurney and Arthur Hochstein, enthusiastically assisted with the book's design and photo editing. I am grateful to many other colleagues past and present, including Josh Tyrangiel, Michael Elliott, Michael Duffy, Nancy Gibbs, Simon Robinson, Amanda Ripley, John Huey, Howard Chua-Eoan, Priscilla Painton, Adi Ignatius, Joe Klein, Andrew Purvis, Ratu Kamlani, and Angela Thornton. Robyn Bacon and Rachael Martin generously housed me during research trips to Southern California. Mike Lucey showed an invigorating interest in this project from the start, purchasing a copy of the book before it was even written. Laura Strickler was a source of inspiration and love throughout.

My sisters, Neethi and Meera, have always been my biggest cheerleaders and critics, as well as my best friends. This book is dedicated to our parents, Rajendra and Queelan, to whom we owe all the blessings in our lives. Though we have surely caused them some grief along the way, their belief in us has never wavered. I hope that this book, in some small portion, serves to redeem their faith.

INDEX

221